STEWARDSHIP
Roots

Ángel M. Rodríguez

Written by Ángel Manuel Rodríguez, ThD
Edited by Patricia Valentino

© 1994
Publication number STW 1050. A Department of Church Ministries publication.
2013 Reprinted and redesigned.
Publication number STW 1050. A Stewardship Ministries Department publication.
ISBN 978-0-9912711-1-5

This material may be translated, printed, or photocopied by any Seventh-day Adventist entity without securing further permission. Republished documents must include the credit line: "Stewardship Ministries Department, General Conference of Seventh-day Adventists, used with permission." Selling this work for profit is prohibited.

Scriptural references are from the Holy Bible, New International Version. Copyright © 1984 International Bible Society. Used by permission of Zondervan Bible Publishers.

Stewardship Ministries Department
General Conference of Seventh-day Adventists
12501 Old Columbia Pike
Silver Spring, MD 20904, USA
gcstewardship@gc.adventist.org
www.adventiststewardship.com
www.Facebook.com/Dynamicstewards

FOREWORD

Stewardship Roots is a reprint of an earlier publication by the General Conference Church Ministries Department under the same title by Dr. Ángel Rodríquez, associate director of the Biblical Research Institute of the General Conference of Seventh-day Adventists at the time of writing.

This resource provides the three papers that were prepared and distributed soon after the Stewardship Summit and Consultation held at Cohutta Springs, Georgia, United States of America, March 20-23, 1994. At Cohutta Springs, Dr. Rodríquez presented two papers—one on the theology of tithe and the other on the theology of offerings. The third paper on the theology of stewardship was written after the summit, and all three documents are included here.

With a renewed interest in Christian stewardship on the part of the General Conference administration and a commitment to play a part in the revival and reformation emphasis of the world church in the 2010-2015 quinquennium, the General Conference Stewardship Ministries Department is pleased to reprint these documents and have them available for the benefit of God's people globally. As a stewardship resource, it is our prayer that the contents of this book will help church members better understand stewardship from the perspective of God. More importantly, we hope that your personal spiritual life will be enriched, your thinking stimulated; that you will find a new sense of appreciation for these important concepts of God's kingdom as you describe your unique relationship with God.

Erika F. Puni
Stewardship Ministries Director
General Conference of Seventh-day Adventists

CONTENTS

Foreword v

Contents vi

1 TOWARD A THEOLOGY OF STEWARDSHIP

Introduction 10

Aspects of the Nature of God 11

   God "Was" 11
   God Is the Creator 12
      The Creator Is Incomparable 12
      The Creator Is Transcendent 13
      The Creator Is Immanent 13
      The Creator Is Owner 14
   God Is Love 15

Aspects of Human Nature 16

   Humans Are Creatures 17
   Humans Are Made in God's Image 18
      A Physical Being 19
      A Spiritual Being 19
      An Intellectual Being 20
      A Social Being 20
   Humans and Dominion Over the World 21

The Fall and Sin 23

   Human Freedom 23
   Sin as Rebellion: Claiming Ownership 25

Sin as Selfishness and Enslavement	26

Salvation and Stewardship — 27

Christ: Image of God and Steward	28
Restoring the Stewards	29
Restoration of the Image of God	33
Stewardship of Creation and Apocalypticism	34

Summary and Conclusions — 35

Follow-Through Discussion — 37

Endnotes — 39

STEWARDSHIP AND THE THEOLOGY OF TITHE

Introduction	42

Tithing in the Old Testament — 43

Genesis 14: Abraham's Tithe	**43**
Tithe Is Based on Income	44
The Recipient of Tithe	45
Theological Basis for Tithing	45
Genesis 28:10-22: Jacob's Tithe	**47**
Jacob's Commitment to God	48
God's Concern for Jacob	48
Jacob Makes a Vow	49
Jacob Worshipped	50
Tithing Legislation	**51**
Leviticus 27:30-33	51
Numbers 18:21-32	53
Deuteronomy 12:6, 11, 17; 14:22-29; 26:12-15	55

Other Old Testament Passages	56
2 Chronicles 31:4-6, 12	57
Amos 4:4	57
Nehemiah 10:38,39; 12:44; 35:5, 12	58
Malachi 3:8-10	60
Tithing in the New Testament	62
Summary and Conclusions	64
Follow-Through Discussion	67
Endnotes	69

STEWARDSHIP AND THE THEOLOGY OF OFFERINGS

Introduction	72
Offerings in the Old Testament	72
Sacrificial Expiatory Offerings	73
Sacrifices as Offerings	74
Burnt Offerings (Leviticus 1:3-17)	74
Peace Offerings (Leviticus 1:3-17)	76
Other Offerings	77
Special Offerings	78
Offerings in the New Testament	81
Jesus and Offerings	82
Offerings and Worship	82
Offerings and Interpersonal Relationships	82
Offerings and Commitment to the Lord	83

Offerings and True Benevolence	84
Offerings and Christian Ministry	84
Paul and Offerings	85
Paul's Reluctance to Accept Offerings	85
Paul as the Recipient of Offerings	87
Paul and the Collection: A Special Offering	89
Motivation for Giving	89
Planned Giving	91
Attitude Toward Giving	92
Purpose of the Collection	93
Offerings in Acts	95
Offering for the Poor	95
Special Offerings	98

Summary and Conclusions   98

Follow-Through Discussion   105

Endnotes   107

TOWARD A THEOLOGY OF STEWARDSHIP

Introduction

Humans are inquisitive creatures involved in a constant search for meaning. This obsession with meaning is not simply an attempt to understand the functional and structural unity of the universe; but rather, a disturbing concern to discover purpose for their existence. Very few things tend to raise a keen sense of interest in humans more than their insatiable curiosity in finding the reason for their existence.

Biblical theology informs us that our origin is located in a divine act of creation and that we were placed on this planet by a loving Creator. He filled our lives with meaning by (among other things) allowing us to assist Him in the administration of the planet. The biblical concept of stewardship is in essence an attempt to clarify the question of purpose for our lives by providing a particular self-understanding based on a personal relationship with the Creator and Redeemer of the human race.

In this document we will examine the theological significance of this concept and the place of this self-understanding within biblical theology. What are the theological roots that nurture the concept of stewardship? How is stewardship related to the biblical view of God, and redemption through Christ? We will explore the theological roots that provided the womb within which this perspective and understanding of human existence were conceived and preserved.

There are at least four main lines of analysis to be pursued in a search for the theological foundation of stewardship, which are: (1) the nature of God, (2) the nature of humans, (3) the Fall and sin, and (4) salvation. We will briefly examine them from the perspective of stewardship.

Aspects of the Nature of God

The nature of God is shrouded in mystery. Philosophers and theologians have tried to penetrate this mystery with very little, if any, success. God's self-revelation in the Scriptures has shed some light on our understanding of His nature, but it continues to be, and will remain, beyond our full comprehension. Let us look at some aspects of God's self-revelation from the perspective of stewardship.

God Was

Whenever the Bible takes us to the very origin and beginning of the universe, several theological statements are implicitly or explicitly made. One of the most important is that God "was." This is implicit in Genesis 1:1: "In the beginning God created." He was, before He created. In John 1:1 this concept is explicitly stated: "In the beginning was the Word." Before anything was brought into existence, God already *was*.

This divine "wasness" means first, that *God is eternal*. There was never a time when God came into existence. If we ask what was there before the beginning, the answer provided by the biblical record is "God." If He was "there" before everything else was brought into existence, then it is impossible to posit a source through which God came into existence. There is no indication in the Scripture to the effect that God "was" because something caused Him to be. The Bible does not speak of a beginning before the beginning. The fact that God "was" points to His eternal nature: He always "was."

Second, the divine "wasness" means that *God is self-sufficient*. Since before the beginning there was nothing else except God; therefore, He is self-sufficient. The Lord exists by Himself. A source of energy was never needed to feed the divine being except Himself. With respect to God, self-sufficiency means that He is self-existent. We should, therefore, agree with those who argue that God is existence in Himself. Life is not something that He possesses; but rather, what He is.

Self-sufficiency means that God is absolutely free and autonomous. Outside Himself there is nothing or no one to whom God should submit. He is His own law. No one can impose obligations on Him or force Him to act in certain specific ways. He does not need anything from anyone because He is self-sufficient. John refers to Him as the "Lord God who is, and who was, and who is to come" (Revelation 1:8; cf 1:4).

The "wasness" of God that we have just described is probably one of the deepest statements we find in Scripture about God, because it is the only one that describes Him for us in Himself, before anything else was brought into existence. A proper understanding of stewardship should be based on the conviction that God is eternal and self-sufficient and that our administration of what He entrusted to us does not have the purpose of enriching Him in any way. Stewardship offers the opportunity to enter into fellowship with this mysterious God who existed from eternity.

God Is the Creator

God introduced Himself to us in the Scriptures as the Creator (Genesis 1:1). If we know that at the beginning He was, it is because we were informed that He was the Creator. God as Creator is "the most fundamental conception we can have of God. That is, creation is that activity of God by means of which we define what we mean by the word 'God.'"[1] Indeed, it would be impossible for us to talk about the mystery of God—that He "was"—apart from the fact that He is the Creator. Our vision of God expands itself when we look at Him as Creator of heaven and earth, and the entire universe.

The Creator Is Incomparable

God as Creator means that there is no one like Him in the created universe. He is essentially different from His creation. He is the Eternal One without beginning, but created beings have a beginning; He is self-existent, but created beings have a derived existence that depends upon proper ecological balances: water, sunlight, oxygen, etc. God is absolutely autonomous, but the creatures depend upon Him for their subsistence. Creatures are finite; only God is infinite in Himself.

Isaiah confronted his people with this penetrating rhetorical question from the lips of the Lord: "To whom will you compare me or count me equal? To whom will you liken me that we may be compared?" (46:5). The questions are addressed to those tempted to idolatry. The Lord seems to be challenging His people: "Have you found another being like me in the created universe? If that is the case, I am ready to be compared to him or her." Then He adds, "Remember the former things, those of long ago; I am God, and there is no other; I am God, and there is none like me" (Isaiah 46:9). Of the divine "species" there is only one unique type. No one from within the created world can occupy His place or claim equality with Him. The Lord is "a supreme, incomparably unique Being."[2]

The Creator Is Transcendent

God as Creator means that He transcends the created universe; He is not part of it. According to Genesis 1, God created through His word. Creation through the spoken word points to God as a transcendent being who mediates His creative activity through the word, while He remains outside creation. It is, therefore, absurd to look for God in the created world. He did not create it out of His essence but through His word. Creation out of nothing denies the validity of pantheism. The created universe is not permeated by the divine. God, the Creator, cannot be circumscribed by that which He created. This fact was recognized by Solomon during the dedication of the temple. During his prayer he said, "But will God really dwell on earth? The heavens, even the highest heaven, cannot contain you" (1 Kings 8:27).

The Creator Is Immanent

God as Creator means that He is willing to enter into the created world. Scholars have pointed out that while Genesis 1 testifies to God's transcendence, Genesis 2 testifies to His immanence. In Genesis 2, God is described as present within creation in full interaction with Adam and Eve.

God's immanence is indispensable for the preservation of creation. The preservation of God's creation is directly dependent on

His care and concern for it. It is, therefore, indispensable for God to remain within His created world once His creative activity is completed. Divine rest on the seventh day points precisely to this significant fact (Genesis 2:2, 3).

Genesis makes clear that creation belongs to the sphere of space and time. God transcends that sphere. However, He chose to enter into that sphere, into the world He created for His creatures. He created a fraction of time within which He made Himself available to His creation. Of course, God remained the Transcendent One. His immanence does not deny His transcendence. God condescends to enter into His creation, making it clear that He has not abandoned it.

The Creator Is Owner

God as Creator means that He owns the universe and everything in it. He is Lord over it and assigns specific tasks to each element of creation (e.g., Genesis 1:14, 26, 29; 2:15, 16). God's ownership of the world is based on His creative activity. The psalmist wrote: "The earth is the Lord's, and everything in it, the world, and all who live in it; for he founded it upon the seas and established it upon the waters" (24:1, 2). God declares, "Every animal of the forest is mine, and the cattle on a thousand hills. I know every bird in the mountains, and the creatures of the field are mine" (Psalm 50:10, 11). God is not only Owner of the material content of this world and of the living beings who populate it, but His ownership is cosmic: "The heavens are yours, and yours also the earth; you founded the world and all that is in it" (89:11). The psalmist knows that "the universe is in Yahweh's hands. To him as the ruler does the world belong."[3]

God as Creator is an indispensable concept in the formulation of the theology of stewardship. *God's incomparability*, His uniqueness, identifies Him as the only One to whom we are accountable as stewards. The universe is not run by opposing forces to which we are equally obliged to serve. There is only one Creator, and He expects our exclusive loyalty.

God's transcendence is a rejection of any attempt to base our practice of stewardship on pantheistic ideas. The natural world is not an extension or a manifestation of the divine. Pantheism cannot provide a theological foundation for the stewardship of the world, because it is rejected by Scripture.

God's immanence testifies to the fact that God's creation is in constant need of His care and concern in order to function harmoniously. The Creator is also the Sustainer of the world. God's condescending presence in the world makes room for humans to participate with Him in the administration and preservation of His creation (e.g., Genesis 2:15).

God's ownership as Creator should remind us constantly of the limits of our function in the world. It is this aspect that defines, perhaps better than any other, the nature of a steward. He or she is never the owner, but the administrator.

God Is Love

Love seems to be used in the Bible to define or describe the essence of God. John's statement, "God is love" (1 John 4:7, 8), is one of the most important descriptions of the nature of God in Scripture. The apostle made that statement in the context of Christ's sacrificial death. According to him, the work of Christ reveals the very essence of God: "He is love." This love is self-giving and totally and absolutely unselfish (e.g., John 3:16). There is nothing outside God that could move or force Him to love. In fact, there is no need for any external motivation, because it is God's very nature to love. This love is "neither based on a felt need in the loving person nor on a desire called forth by some attractive feature(s) in the loved one."[4] It was this understanding of God's love that led Paul to say, "God demonstrates his own love for us in this: While we were still sinners, Christ died for us" (Romans 5:8).

God is love means that every one of His actions originates with and is motivated by love. Election is based on His love (Deuteronomy 7:7, 8) as well as redemption (Isaiah 43:4; 63:9). He loves not only His people (Deuteronomy 33:3), but also the alien (10:18). The revelation of God's love reaches its deepest dimension of meaning in the incarnation, ministry, death, and resurrection of Jesus. His love for sinners is not motivated by the misery of their sinful condition, but by the fact that God is love, and it is this great fact that moves Him to love sinners in spite of their sin.[5] In order for God's love to express itself, another person is needed. Love occurs among individuals who receive, give, and respond. This raises the important question of the nature of God's love before creation. Unselfish love is a possibility only if there is another person to whom it can be expressed. Before creation, when God "was," He was alone. Was His love then selfish? Was God's nature altered after He created intelligent creatures capable of receiving and giving love? Christian theologians have given a resounding *no* as an answer to those questions. The Bible tells of only one God who is love. Unselfish love, therefore, belongs to the eternal nature of God. His nature has not experienced change; He is what He has always been: "Love."

Christian theologians have rightly argued that unselfish love found eternal expression within God in the mystery of the Trinity. The relations between the Father, the Son, and the Holy Spirit were conditioned by the essence of unselfish love, which was common to each one of them (e.g., John 14:31; 5:20).[6] Unselfish love requires an encounter of distinct persons, and that is exactly what we find in the mystery of a triune God. Throughout eternity the Father loved the Son and the Spirit, the Son loved the Father and the Spirit, and the Spirit loved the Father and the Son.[7]

That same loving God brought the universe into existence. His eternal love moved Him to create: "The work of creation was a manifestation of His love."[8] Creation is good because it was brought into existence by a loving God (Genesis 1:31). Ultimate reality is personal and unselfish.

A clear understanding of God's love protects stewardship from falling into a legalistic mode. A faithful steward is not one who is seeking to motivate God to love him or her. The love of God is eternal and defines the natural way He feels and acts toward His creation. Stewardship finds its motivating force and model in the unselfish and caring love of God.

Aspects of Human Nature

It is probably right to suggest that humans are the most intricate and mysterious creatures in the known universe. We, unlike any other created being on the planet, are capable of perceiving ourselves as wonderful and fascinating. The mystery of our presence in the universe becomes absolutely impenetrable if we ignore the information about our origin provided to us through God's special revelation in Scripture. We should review some of that data.

Humans Are Creatures

Genesis 1:27 states: "God created man . . . male and female he created them." This is a statement of paramount importance in the formulation of a biblical anthropology. Humans are created beings; we are part of the created world. First, this means that we had a beginning. We are not eternal; we do not belong to the divine. Our mode of existence is essentially different from God's. He always "was," but we came into existence. Our role within the universe is one of a created being.

Second, humans are finite beings. Their existence is derived and *in itself* lacks self-sufficiency. We are not self-contained beings who can produce our own source of existence to preserve ourselves. Since we were brought into existence, we can also be returned to nothingness, our existence can come to an end. However, although the preservation of our existence is ultimately beyond ourselves, we are expected to work with the Creator in the preservation of our lives. We are, therefore, stewards of life.

Third, viewing humans as creatures means that they exist within time and space. Both of those elements are indicated in the creation narrative. Adam and Eve were created on the sixth day, during a particular fraction of time. They were time-conditioned from the very beginning. They were brought into existence within a particular place—namely, the garden. Obviously, the space is really the rest of the created world. Their home was the flora and fauna, the rest of the universe. If the space where we exist is ruined, our existence is jeopardized. The stewardship of creation is of vital importance.

Humans live within time. Events and actions succeed each other; what was belongs to the past, and it is impossible for us to go back and relive it. Only the present is, and it lasts just fractions of seconds because it is constantly transmuted into the past. We always have the future, what is not yet. Since there is future time, humans live in hope, constantly facing the challenge of self-development. Time is, therefore, one of the most important aspects of the created universe. Time forms, changes, and modifies us. The way we use it determines to a large extent whom we become. The proper administration of time is undoubtedly one of our most serious responsibilities. Living within time and space is not a limitation but rather the mode of our existence and provides us with freedom to move within that continuum in order to be what we may choose to be.

Finally, to be a created being means that we are not the result of impersonal forces within the created world, but the result of a creative act of love. Our existence is a manifestation of God's selfless love, an act of grace. We were created by Him, because in His love God saw that this was good. Divine love, grace, and freedom brought into existence an intelligent creature who was part of the created world and yet different. This creature was capable of receiving and returning love.

Humans Are Made in God's Image

The uniqueness of the human race is located in the fact that we were created in God's image (Genesis 1:27). The creation of Adam and Eve does not follow the same pattern used by God in the creation of the world. He spoke, and the natural world came into existence. In this particular case, speech preceded existence. In the case of Adam and Eve, the spoken word is not present. God's voice addressed them only after their creation (Genesis 1:29, 30; 2:16). They were singled out by God as objects of His speech. (In other words, humans are creatures to whom God can relate, whom He can address as persons.) Only they, within the created world, could relate to God in personal terms. This aspect of our human nature makes it possible for us to be partners with God in stewardship.

For centuries theologians have discussed the meaning of the image of God in humans. Different suggestions have been given, but today there seems to be a general agreement on the belief that the image of God is not something that we have but something that we are.[9] God's image in us is not located in one aspect of our personality but in the totality of our being. At creation, God's image was reflected in every aspect of Adam and Eve. We will explore some of these aspects from a wholistic point of view.

A Physical Being

The first thing we notice about a human being is that he or she is a physical structure that can be perceived by the eye and touched by others. If the whole person was created in God's image, the physical body should also express it: "In the beginning, man was created in the likeness of God, not only in character, but in form and feature."[10]

The very fact that God created us as physical entities indicates that the human body is good, thus rejecting Greek anthropological dualism, which denies the value of the human body. The preservation of the body is a dual responsibility of God and people. He provided everything Adam and Eve needed to preserve their bodies in perfect condition, and assigned them a specific diet that they were expected to consume (Genesis 1:29).

The stewardship of our bodies is based on the fact that God created us as physical beings. Our bodies are not something we have but something we are.[11] Our bodies and what we are, are inseparable. God expects us to administer them to His glory (1 Corinthians 6:20).

A Spiritual Being

Humans are more than matter. We have the capacity to listen to God and to answer back. Apparently, no other creature on this planet seems to have that ability. There is a communality of language between God and humans that makes it possible for them to enter into fellowship and to establish a meaningful relationship.

Humans are essentially religious persons. We come to understand ourselves particularly in terms of our relationship with God. The first relationship Adam and Eve established was with their Creator. When Adam was created, Eve was not present; and when she was created, he was not present. The first image each one of them captured was the one of the Creator. Every other relationship was determined by that primary one, and apart from it they would not have been able to understand themselves or the rest of creation.

But the encounter between God and humans was not going to be restricted to the moment of creation. They needed God for their subsistence and for the satisfaction of the need of a personal relationship with Him. Hence, the transcendental God decided to remain with them in time and space. It is in God's gracious willingness to come and dwell with us that the stewardship of our spiritual life was originally born.

An Intellectual Being

God gave Adam and Eve rational abilities through which they could derive a deeper understanding of Him, themselves, and the created world. Through fully sanctified reason, humans were going to be able to control their emotions and passions, to learn, and to develop all kind of skills.

In the Garden of Eden God assigned Adam work that required the use of his intellectual capacities (Genesis 2:15). Particularly, God asked Adam to assign names to the animals (2:19, 20). In the Bible a name is an extremely important matter, because it is a reflection of the character of the person who bears it. Giving names to the animals implies that Adam was to observe and analyze their behavior in order to name them properly. This was a scientific study of nature. He was exploring God's creation, systematizing it, understanding its order and harmony. He was putting the skills and talents God had given him at the service of God and of nature. It is there that the theological basis for the stewardship of our talents is to be located. God endowed us with the capacity to develop skills and to acquire new knowledge, and these were to be put into His service.

A Social Being

Humans cannot exist meaningfully in total isolation. Our capacity to interact with others is a manifestation of the fact that we were created by God in His image. It has been suggested that Genesis 1:27 points to that aspect of the image of God in us: "God created man in his own image, in the image of God he created him; male and female he created them." "Man" is a plurality of persons, a unity formed by a female and a male. Some scholars have located in that plurality a manifestation of the image of God. Male and female are the image, because they together are one.[12] A plurality defines "man" and God. The basic idea is that the image of God in "man" includes a plurality that allows for inter-human relations in a "similar" way that the plurality in God makes possible intra-trinitarian relations. Humans, like God, are relational beings, because true love always needs another person to express itself.

Apart from our relationship with God, one of the most important social interactions takes place within the family structure. God instructed Adam and Eve about this fundamental relationship, describing for them the nature of marriage. Marriage has a unitive (Genesis 2:24) and a procreative purpose (1:28). Unity in love can reach its fullest dimension within marriage. At the same time, God gave humans the privilege to contribute with Him to the perpetuation of the human race. This is the result of our social nature and, particularly, of the interaction and commitment in love between the male and female. It is out of the positive social interaction in the family that the possibility of further meaningful relationships with others can develop.

As social beings, we are particularly responsible for the stewardship of our social influence at home, the church, and society at large. Treating others with respect, concern, and love is a test of the stewardship of our social life. The values and principles of our commitment to the Lord should have a direct and positive impact on our social interaction.

Humans and Dominion Over the World

According to Genesis 1:28, Adam and Eve were to subdue the earth and to have dominion over the fauna. Thus was defined their relationship to the rest of creation. Undoubtedly, in that task the image of God was revealed in a special way. God has given humans power and authority: "Every human being, created in the image of God, is endowed with a power akin to that of the Creator—individuality, power to think and to do."[13]

The Hebrew verb "to have dominion" is used in the Old Testament to designate the power of the king over his people.[14] In Genesis this power is granted to humankind and is limited only to the animal world.[15] We are commissioned here "to rule nature as a benevolent king, acting as God's representative over them and therefore treating them in the same way as God who created them."[16] The fact that humans were vegetarians indicates that the destruction of animal life was not contemplated in the granting of dominion over them.[17] The dominion was a positive one, having to do with "securing the well-being of every other creature and bringing the promise of each to full fruition."[18]

The verb "to subdue" the land should be understood in terms of Genesis 2:5, 15, as taking care of the land. The idea of using that power to exploit nature is ruled out by the context in which the goodness of creation is to be understood in terms of its perfect harmony and unity. Humans were not to upset the order established by God but to respect and preserve it.

The dominion of humans over nature reveals an important function of humankind as God's image: They are representatives of God within the created world. We have been told that man "was placed, as God's representative, over the lower orders of being. They cannot understand or acknowledge the sovereignty of God, yet they were made capable of loving and serving man."[19] God delegated to Adam and Eve, as His representatives, the responsibility of administering the rest of creation. God appointed humans to be stewards of the world.[20]

The command to have dominion over the world reveals something about the nature of creation. It presupposes a non-mythological understanding of nature. Ancient mythologies often tell about divine trees, rivers, animals, earth, etc. When confronted by them, humans were not to explore them but to submit to them. Such ideas are absent from the biblical text: "there is neither a divine earth, nor divine beasts, nor divine constellations, nor any other divine spheres basically inaccessible to man."[21] There is nothing superior to humankind in the created order.

Human dominion over creation implies that nature is finite and dependent upon the care of humans. This element of dependency seems to belong to the very nature of creation. The dependence is, of course, mutual. Nature depends upon the kingly ruling of loving persons in order to reveal its fruitfulness, greatness, and beauty. But human existence is intrinsically related to it. God determined that their existence be mutually dependent, although, ultimately, they both depended upon Him.

We conclude that from God's perspective humans are stewards of the natural world. This is possible because there is nothing divine or sacred in nature. This concept is of great significance for people interested in ecological issues. Our concern for the well-being of the planet is not to be based on its presumed sanctity, but on the fact that God appointed people as stewards of the world.

The Fall and Sin

It is sometimes difficult for us to conceive, or even imagine, a time in the history of this planet when there was perfect harmony on earth. The divine intention was that humans, united to God in undivided commitment to Him, would continue to have dominion over the planet, exploring it and preserving it in all of its beauty and greatness. It is clear that stewardship belongs to God's original intention and design for the mission of the human race on our planet. It served to define the fundamental responsibility of the human family toward God and toward the created order. But the intrusion of sin upset the divine plan.

Human Freedom

In Christian theology the concepts of sin and freedom are closely interconnected. The biblical narrative of the Fall provides support for this conclusion. The creation account presupposes that humans were created as free agents. In that context freedom probably means that they had the ability to become that which God intended them to be. It was freedom to realize themselves, to bring into fruition their human potentiality as creatures of God. Therefore, human freedom was a reality only if humans would remain in a harmonious relationship with God. It is to this type of freedom that Genesis 2:16, 17, refers: "And the Lord God commanded the man, `You are free to eat from any tree in the garden; but you must not eat from the tree of the knowledge of good and evil, for when you eat of it you will surely die.'"

These two verses define the true nature of freedom and

establish its boundaries. We have a positive, permissive command followed by a limitation. Adam and Eve are free to eat of any tree in the garden, thus satisfying their need for food. The Lord provided for all their basic needs, and by listening to His command, life was preserved. The prohibition, "You shall not eat of the tree of good and evil," in a sense, made them aware of the extent of their freedom. They had the freedom to reject fellowship with God. Adam and Eve were free to say "no" to God and to the life that came from Him.[22]

Without that possibility, Adam and Eve were not free but prisoners on this planet. They would have been created to live in this world without an alternative or a way out. God brought them into existence without consulting them, without giving them the freedom to decide whether they wanted to exist. (Obviously, such a thing would have been impossible, because freedom of choice implies existence and consciousness.) God simply brought them into existence and then gave them the freedom to say yes or no to Him and to life. God's real intention is for humans to choose life and fellowship with Him. Hence, the negative command. Its purpose was to preserve Adam and Eve alive by their choice of the gift of life. Their freedom was being tested: "They could obey and live, or disobey and perish."[23] It was their responsibility to decide whether to return to nothingness or to enjoy endless life and freedom in total harmony, obedience, and trust in the Creator.

The name of the tree whose fruit Adam and Eve were not to eat is an interesting one, "tree of the knowledge of good and evil." Many suggestions have been given as to the meaning of that phrase,[24] but it should probably be interpreted in terms of Genesis 3:22, "And the Lord God said, 'The man has now become like one of us, knowing good and evil.'" Knowing good and evil is a type of knowledge that belongs exclusively to God. The phrase does not designate the ability to know everything, because humans were never created to become omniscient. What the phrase emphasizes is the possibility for humans to decide for themselves what is in their best interest and what is not.[25] It seems to be a phrase used to express the idea of absolute moral autonomy and decision-making without a sense of accountability. God said to Adam and Eve that to have that experience is to reject Him and to choose death. The tree was, therefore, a symbol of self-determination and total independence, which would lead inexorably to death, because it would be a rejection of the gift of life. In essence, this would be ultimate rebellion against God.

Sin as Rebellion: Claiming Ownership

The serpent, being the most clever animal in the garden, became an instrument of evil (Genesis 3:1). This is somewhat surprising because he is one of God's good creatures (1:31). It is interesting to notice that during the judgment scene described in 3:9-14, God asked Adam and Eve to explain their behavior and give reasons for it. Yet, no question was addressed to the serpent. There was no dialogue between God and the serpent, because there was nothing to explain; sin is inexplicable, irrational. Sin can only be condemned, and that was exactly what God did.

The serpent, during his conversation with Eve, confronted her with the possibility of a new self-understanding and a new worldview. The message was appealing and persuasive. He introduced himself with a question that forced Eve to react. God was misquoted and Eve decided to defend Him, but in the process she became vulnerable. The serpent became more aggressive and openly contradicted God's statement about the result of eating from the tree of the knowledge of good and evil (3:4, 5).

According to the serpent, death was not a threat to the creature, because the creature could not die. The creature could only move from one lower level of existence to a higher one. Eating of the fruit of the tree, he argued, would open up new vistas of self-understanding to Eve and her husband. She would be a step closer to the divine; in fact, she would be like God, knowing good and evil. "Yes," said the serpent, "you can have total self-determination, you can be your own master, you can be the source of your own life."

The serpent proceeded to question God's goodness by suggesting that God was limiting the full enjoyment of life by Adam and Eve by requiring them to depend on Him. They could attain those new dimensions of existence through autonomy and independence from God. All they had to do was to reject their role as stewards of God and become owners of life.

Eve wanted to grow, to develop herself, and to fully realize her potential. It was the Lord who put the desire in her heart for wisdom. But she and her husband misused their freedom and overstepped their limits. They both rejected their status as stewards of God in order to become owners. They ate of the fruit of the tree, not because they were rejecting God's gift of life, but because they wanted to appropriate and enjoy it in total independence from God. They were interested in breaking away from their creatureliness to be like God. They were deceived by the serpent, because what he offered them was irreal. They had, in fact, chosen death and not life. In eating the fruit, humanity lost its stewardship of the world.

Sin as Selfishness and Enslavement

The decision of Adam and Eve was an act of rebellion that brought disruption into the world, affecting the harmony of creation. After their sin, the first thing they experienced was shame in front of each other. They saw each other as strangers, and, consequently, their social life was no longer the same. The internal spiritual disruption was reflected in the rejection of the other.

We apprehend the other primarily through the body. Social life and interaction are impossible outside the body. To feel ashamed when facing another person means that interpersonal relations are no longer harmonious. Adam and Eve wanted full autonomy, independence from God, but they did not realize that such a desire would also mean independence from each other. Selfishness had been born in their hearts, and from then on it would characterize the human race.

Interestingly, even though they claimed independence from God, Adam and Eve were still accountable to Him for their actions. They hid from the Lord because they had become unfaithful stewards. The Lord judged them and found them guilty (Genesis 3:8-19). The Lord always looks at humans as stewards, because that was what He appointed them to be. A corrupted and selfish nature would not justify the rejection of that role.

Because of their sin, Adam and Eve became *slaves of sin*. Paul indicated that humans become slaves of the one whom they choose to obey (Romans 6:16). The human race chose to serve sin and was enslaved by it (6:17), being under its power and captive to the law of sin (7:14, 23). Humans cannot submit to the law of God; it is impossible for them to please God (Romans 8:7, 8). There is a fundamental inability in them to serve God. Human nature was corrupted at its very center, bringing with it a natural hostility toward God (8:7), becoming weakened, and with a natural tendency to sin. This nature, possessed by sin, controlled the human race (8:9). Because of this slavery to sin, it was impossible for humans to be faithful stewards of God.

Sin, as a rebellion against God, not only brought selfishness and slavery, but it also *affected the image of God* in humanity. "For all have sinned and fall short of the glory of God" (Romans 3:23). As a result of sin, our spiritual and moral natures have been corrupted. In fact, no aspect of the human being has been left untouched by sin. Yet, the image has not been totally obliterated (cf Genesis 9:6).[26] It is true that humans have "defaced the image of God" in their soul by a corrupt way of life,[27] but "traces" of it still "remain upon every soul."[28] The corruption of the image meant also that nature itself "was subjected to frustration . . . bondage . . . decay" (Romans 8:20, 21).

The role of humans as stewards of God was drastically damaged through sin. Sin, as rebellion against God, characterized humans who then proclaimed themselves owners of everything, and, in particular, of their own lives, which they attempted to preserve through their own efforts. Hence, they became slaves of sin, unable to be what the Lord intended them to be. The restoration of humans to their original status as stewards of God would require a plan that would address the issues of rebellion, selfishness, slavery, and the restoration of the image of God.

Salvation and Stewardship

We have noticed that stewardship in the Old Testament originates with the gift of creation and life. God brought into existence intelligent human life and assigned it the role of representing Him in this world. Stewardship in the New Testament finds its basis in God's gift of salvation through Christ. In both cases, the one who gives is the Lord, and the one who receives and administers is the Lord's steward, who was created and is re-created through and in Christ.

Christ: Image of God and Steward

In order to release the planet from the power of sin, God needed a faithful steward, one who would represent Him properly as His image in a world alienated from Him. This happened in Christ Jesus.

Several passages in the New Testament refer to Jesus as the image of God. One of the most significant is Colossians 1:15: "He is the image of the invisible God, the firstborn over all creation." The passage is alluding to Genesis 2:16, where Adam and Eve are described as the image of God who represented Him to the lower order of creation.[29] Now, it is Christ who is described as the image of God. The title "Firstborn of Creation" is used to indicate His supremacy as representative of God. It emphasizes His uniqueness as agent of creation and as Lord over it.[30] In the context of Colossians the representation of God in Christ is indeed a revelation of God to His creatures. This thought is clearly expressed in 2 Corinthians 2:2, where the expression "image of God" stresses the function of Christ as the revealer of God's glory. He bore the image of God not as something given to Him but as what He was in essence. Christ was fully God, "the radiance of God's glory and the exact representation of his being, sustaining all things by his powerful word" (Hebrews 1:3).

This man Jesus, the image of God, is the true Steward of God. John states, "The Father loves the Son and has placed everything in his hands" (3:35). Placing everything in the hands of someone means giving him or her power and authority over them.[31] In other places Jesus testified, "All things have been committed to me by my Father" (Matthew 11:27; Luke 10:22). The Father entrusted Jesus with responsibilities that He was going to fulfill as faithful Steward and Son. The relationship was centered in mutual love. The reference in those passages is primarily to Jesus' work as Savior. This was the most important task ever assigned by God to any of His stewards; He assigned it to His own Son.

Christ, as a steward of God, is administering for Him the plan of salvation for Him. It was God's plan to unite everything in and through Christ. The plan was "put into effect" by Christ Himself (Ephesians

1:10). "Put into effect" is the translation of the Greek *eis oikonomian* = lit., "for administration." The term *oikonomia* is the Greek noun usually translated "stewardship, administration." Paul, in Ephesians, seems to be suggesting that Christ "is the steward through whom God is working out his plan for the world—a plan that is in process and that will be culminated when the times will have reached their fulfillment (lit., 'in the fullness of time')."[32] Christ, as steward, is in charge of "God's house," the church (Hebrews 3:6); but is also bringing reconciliation to the universe (Colossians 1:20).

Jesus submitted Himself to the Father and obediently followed His instructions concerning how to put into effect the plan of salvation (cf John 17:2, 4). He was a faithful steward who remained loyal to God where Adam and Eve had failed. While Adam and Eve sought independence from God by trying to be like Him, Christ "being in very nature God, did not consider equality with God something to be grasped, but made himself nothing, taking the very nature of a servant, being made in human likeness. And being found in appearance as a man, he humbled himself and became obedient to death—even death on a cross!" (Philippians 2:6-8).

Christ is a unique steward because, in order to preserve the life of those entrusted to Him, He gave his life for them (Romans 5:6). He gave everything He had in order to preserve the human race, for which He assumed responsibility as God's steward. This was not expected from any other steward of God. When Moses offered himself to die in place of Israel, God rejected his offer (Exodus 32:31, 33). This task was preserved for the God-man, Jesus Christ, the Son of God. He, who was rich, became poor "so that you through his poverty might become rich" (2 Corinthians 8:9). In Philippians Paul refers to that same experience by declaring Christ "made himself nothing" (2:7). Christ emptied Himself of His right to use His divinity, and instead submitted Himself to His Father's will.[33] This was His role in life, and, as such, He fulfilled His responsibility as God's steward.

Restoring the Stewards

A Christian is a person who has recognized and accepted that Christ is the very image of God and is now willing to be conformed to that image. But before that could take place, the alienation caused by sin should be removed. The individual is to be restored to peace with God; accept his or her proper function in the world; stop striving selfishly for self-preservation; and be redeemed from the power of sin, which makes it impossible to be a faithful steward of God. All of that is possible through Christ, who reconciled us to God, made possible our justification by faith, and redeemed us from the power of sin.

The *spirit of rebellion* located at the center of our fallen nature can be overcome only through the work of Christ, which made possible our *reconciliation with God*. Reconciliation is a manifestation of God's self-sacrificing love (Romans 5:8-10). In Christ, God was reconciling the world to Himself (2 Corinthians 5:19). This seems to mean that because of the work of Christ, God set aside His wrath against us as sinners, making possible our reconciliation with Him.[34] By taking the initiative God revealed His love, thus disarming us of our spirit of rebellion and calling us to be reconciled with Him (5:20). This is possible because God made Christ, "who had no sin to be made sin for us, so that in him we might become the righteousness of God" (5:21).

At the cross God showed us that there is no reason to be at war with Him, because He has always loved us. Reconciliation is a recognition and acceptance of our place in the universe. It is the rejection on our part of any idea or attempt to usurp God's authority or His claim of ownership. Paul introduces his discussion on the meaning of reconciliation in Colossians by saying, "For by him [Christ] all things were created: things in heaven and on earth, visible and invisible, whether thrones or powers or rulers or authorities; all things were created by him and for him" (1:16). Creation was accomplished by God through Christ, and therefore *everything belongs to the Savior*. Even more, He is the One who holds the universe together (1:17). Yet, it was He who took our place, dying on the cross because of our rebellion, making possible our reconciliation with God (2 Corinthians 5:14, 15, 21; Ephesians 2:3-5). Reconciliation implies a recognition of God's ownership of the universe and of our role as stewards of the Lord. Those who have been reconciled "should no longer live for themselves but for him who died for them and was raised again" (2 Corinthians 5:15).

Living for ourselves is an obvious manifestation of our

selfishness, which makes it practically impossible to be a true steward of God. Since Adam and Eve fell into sin, humans have been constantly attempting to preserve their lives through their own efforts. This dimension of sin was dealt with by Christ. Selfishness makes us ineffective administrators of God's blessings, because whatever we receive from God we appropriate for ourselves in order to feel secure and to make sure that we will be able to enjoy life on this planet by ourselves. Such selfishness has no concern for others, because we are totally obsessed with the thought of self-preservation.

The solution to this sinful human condition is found in Christ's sacrificial death on the cross, which made it possible for us to be justified by faith in Him (Romans 3:21-26). Justification means that we have been acquitted in God's court, because Christ took our place, dying for us. The preservation of our lives is no longer to be our concern but God's. He through Christ gave us life freely as a gift of grace (5:18). Before coming to Christ we were spiritually dead in our sins and transgressions (Ephesians 2:1). But through Christ God made us alive through the revelation of His grace: "For it is by grace you have been saved, through faith—and this not from yourselves, it is the gift of God" (2:8).

Christ's sacrificial death showed that God's self-sacrificing love overcomes evil. Christ gave His life in order to preserve ours, showing clearly that life is preserved when it is surrendered to God in a trusting and living relationship (Matthew 16:25). Apart from Christ there is no life in us (John 6:53; 10:10). It is only through justification by faith that we have life (Romans 5:18). Consequently, the center of our lives is no longer self but Christ. Now, we live for Him and to His glory (Romans 6:10-11). Paul describes, in very vivid language, the dethronement of selfishness in his life through the work of Christ on the cross, saying: "I have been crucified with Christ and I no longer live, but Christ lives in me. The life I live in the body, I live by faith in the Son of God, who loved me and gave himself for me" (Galatians 2:20).

Finally, our freedom from the enslaving power of sin is real because God, in Christ, redeemed us from it. Jesus stated, "For even the Son of Man did not come to be served, but to serve, and to give his life as a ransom for many" (Mark 10:45). Sin made us slaves, unable to serve God and others (Romans 6:6), and destined for eternal death

(6:23). On the cross we were liberated from sin and death: "Since the children have flesh and blood, he too shared in their humanity so that by his death he might destroy him who holds the power of death—that is, the devil—and free those who all their lives were held in slavery by their fear of death" (Hebrews 2:14, 15). God in Christ paid the price of our redemption with "the precious blood of Christ, a lamb without blemish or defect" (1 Peter 1:19).

Those who believe in Christ belong to Him. Paul wrote to the Corinthians, "You are not your own; you were bought at a price. Therefore honor God with your body" (1 Corinthians 6:19, 20). Redemption means that we are no longer under the power of sin because our lives were "bought back" by God through Christ. Our lives are not ours, but God has given us the freedom to administer them properly in order to become what He originally intended us to be—namely, His stewards. This is possible through the gift of the Spirit given by God to those who believe in Christ. They "do not live according to the sinful nature but according to the Spirit" (Romans 8:4). Such individuals "have their minds set on what that nature desires" (8:5), because the Spirit lives in them (8:9).

A theology of stewardship is based not only on the concept of creation and what God intended us to be, but also on salvation through Christ, which makes it possible for us, in spite of our sin, to become what God intended us to be. Through the power of the gospel God undid the damage caused by sin (Romans 1:16,17). Through reconciliation in Christ, our rebellion against God came to an end, and we recognized God as the Creator, Sustainer, Preserver, and Owner of the universe. Once more we found our proper place in God's plan to be that of a servant to a loving God and not the illegal owner of the world and of our lives. Through justification by faith our blind concern for the self-preservation of our lives comes to an end by recognizing that in Christ our lives have been preserved freely by a loving God. Selfishness expired at the cross through the revelation of God's self-sacrificing love. Redemption restored freedom from the power of sin to us, making it possible for us, through the ruling power of the Spirit, to become faithful stewards of the Lord. We reach the highest level of self-realization through service to God and to others.

Restoration of the Image of God

It is through the work of Christ and the power of the Spirit that God's image is to be restored in us. It has always been God's purpose that repentant sinners "be conformed to the image of His Son," becoming His brothers (Romans 8:29). The verb *conform* points to sanctification as "a progressive conformity to Christ, who is the *eikon* [image] of God, and so as a progressive renewal of the believer into that likeness of God."[35] This is clearly indicated in 2 Corinthians 3:18, where we are described as "being transformed into his likeness with ever-increasing glory." The new self of the believer "is being renewed in knowledge in the image of its Creator" (Colossians 3:10). The full restoration of the image of Christ in us will be consummated at the second coming of Christ (1 Corinthians 15:49). But what is important for us is that the image is being reestablished in us now in Christ, and that, consequently, we are being restored to our original function as stewards of God.

The most important responsibility of the Christian steward in the New Testament is the proper "administration" of God's grace, that is to say, the proclamation of the gospel (1 Corinthians 9:17; Ephesians 3:2, 9), or of "the secret things of God" revealed to us in Christ (1 Corinthians 4:1). We, like Christ, participate in the administration of God's plan of salvation (Colossians 1:25). This includes not only proclaiming the good news, but also living up to its sanctifying demands for our lives.

In addition, we are also stewards of God's gifts. In a sense this is part of the administration of God's grace, because within the church His grace manifests itself especially in the bestowal of gifts to every believer (1 Peter 4:10). In this setting stewardship characterizes itself by a disposition to serve others. When Peter calls the Christian community to administer faithfully the gifts given by God, he is suggesting that we are stewards of everything we have, because all of it was given to us by God. Every Christian possession is to be administered to the glory of God. This would include everything God gave us at creation, including our bodies (1 Corinthians 6:19, 20) and our financial resources (see next two chapters). The Christian who is persuaded that everything was created and redeemed by God through Christ and, therefore, everything belongs to the Lord, will never perceive himself or herself as owner, but always as a steward of God and Christ.

Stewardship of Creation and Apocalypticism

The emphasis of the New Testament on apocalyptic eschatology, which announces the destruction of the wicked and the conflagration of the world (e.g., 2 Peter 3:8-10), may tend to suggest that our responsibility as stewards of God does not include a definite concern for the natural world. Why should we care about that which will be destroyed by God at the eschaton?

Such a conclusion would be a serious and terrible mistake. We should notice that the New Testament describes God as seriously interested in the natural world. He feeds the birds of the air, who cannot sow or reap (Matthew 6:26), cares for the life of the sparrow (10:29), and clothes the grass of the field with beauty (6:28-30). Nowhere in the Bible is the natural world described as essentially evil. Rather, it is good because God brought it into existence. God's concern for it is exemplary for His stewards. They are to treat with respect and care that which belongs to their Lord. Only the wicked destroy the earth, and the Lord in due time will destroy them (Revelation 11:18).

The apocalyptic conflagration of the natural world is to be understood as an act of redemption that leads to the renewal of creation and not to its extinction. It is a transitional point from a world infected by sin and evil to one liberated from it. It is not the denial of nature but a reaffirmation of its goodness. The experience of nature can be contrasted with that of the wicked powers. They will be totally destroyed, extinguished from God's universe, without any possibility of a re-creation. They will be condemned as being essentially evil. Not so with the natural world. The final conflagration is its liberation.

Paul, in Romans 8:19-22, personifies the natural world and indicates that because of its solidarity with humans, it has been affected by their experience in two ways. First, it has been "infected" by the sin humans brought into the world. It has been subjected to frustration but "not by its own choice" (verse 20). Therefore, nature is amoral but is trapped in the consequences of human sin. It is now in a state of bondage and decay (verse 19). Second, nature lives in the expectation of the fulfillment of the promise of the future redemption to be experienced by humans at the eschaton. Christ came bringing freedom to those who believe in Him and together with them nature looks forward to the consummation of that freedom. Nature is not expecting a future participation in the eternal destruction of the wicked, but rather, "into the glorious freedom of the children of God" (verse 21). For Paul, the present condition of nature is a transitory one, which will have an (historical) end "in the liberation of creation to the freedom awaited by the children of God."[36]

The apocalyptic hope also includes the natural world. The liberation of God's people includes within it the liberation of the natural world. This positive perspective of nature is a motivating force for the Christian steward to care for the natural world and to act responsibly before God by preserving and protecting it. Their fates are mysteriously intertwined.

Summary and Conclusions

Our exploration of the theological meaning of stewardship began with a discussion of the nature of God. Before anything came into existence, He already was. This means that He is eternal and self-sufficient. Our function as stewards is not to enrich or provide for His needs, because He is self-sufficient. Stewardship is the privilege of being in partnership with this mysterious and sublime God. As Creator, He is Unique, Incomparable, Transcendental, Immanent, and Owner. It is to this only God that we are accountable as stewards. His transcendence protects stewardship from viewing nature as divine, while His immanence shows His concern for creation and makes it possible for us to be His stewards. God the Creator is the Owner reminding us that we should never claim ownership. God is described also as "love." Stewardship will spoil itself if understood as the attempt of the steward to obtain God's love. God loves us because He is love. His love becomes a model to be followed by the steward as he or she administers God's gifts.

Our discussion of human nature pointed out that we are creatures of God. In the preservation of our lives, we work together with God. We are stewards of our lives. Since we live within time and space, we are also stewards of our time and our environment. We were created in God's image. This image is what we are and finds expression in every aspect of our being. We are, therefore, stewards of our bodies, of our spiritual life, of our mental and intellectual capacities, and of our social being. Created in the image of God, we were given dominion over nature. We were made responsible to administer it for the Lord as His representatives.

The biblical doctrine of sin points to the fact that our function as stewards of God was seriously upset through sin. Sin as rebellion means that humans claimed ownership of their lives and of the world. This resulted in a selfish concern for self-preservation. We became slaves of sin, unable to function as faithful servants of the Lord.

The doctrine of salvation through Christ explains how we were restored to our original function as stewards of God. In a world alienated from God, He sent His Son as the true Steward, who was in essence the "image of God" in this world of sin. Christ became the steward in the plan of salvation. In order to preserve the life of those entrusted to Him, He gave His own life for them. His sacrificial death reconciled us with God, making it possible to bring to an end our rebellion against the Creator, who is once more recognized as the true and only Owner of the universe and of our lives. Our selfish concern for the preservation of our lives comes to an end when we accept Christ's death as the means of our justification. God in Christ is the One who preserves our lives, and we can trust Him and set aside our selfishness. Freedom from the enslaving power of sin is a reality because Christ redeemed us from it on the cross. We belong to Him through redemption. Now through the sanctifying power of the Spirit we can be transformed into the image of the Son of God; we can be reinstated as stewards of God.

One of our primary responsibilities as stewards of God is the stewardship of the gospel, which includes preaching it and submitting our lives to it. But we are also stewards of all God's gifts to us. We are in a special way stewards of nature. Apocalyptic eschatology should not diminish our concern for the natural world. We look forward to the consummation of our freedom from the presence of sin and to the restoration of the natural world.

TOWARD A THEOLOGY OF STEWARDSHIP
Follow-through Discussion on Stewardship

1. What is your overall reaction to the move toward establishing a "theology of stewardship"? Do you concur with the four main lines of analysis for the theological foundation of stewardship? What suggestions do you have?

   (This is just a beginning! We would appreciate your written response, reaction or ideas. Email them to: gcstewardship@gc.adventist.org.)

2. What relationship does the "wasness" of God have with the biblical foundations of stewardship?

3. Discuss the essential differences between God the Creator and His created beings.

4. How is humanity's election motivated by God's love?

5. What unique characteristics do people possess because we are created in "God's image"?

6. Explain how the words "and let them have dominion" describe the power and authority given to humans by God.

7. Discuss how the concepts of sin and freedom are closely interconnected in Christian theology and sacred history.

8. Because of Adam and Eve's rebellion against God, what sinful characteristics did the human race inherited?

9. What is the relationship between stewardship and the doctrine of salvation in Christ?

10. Discuss whether it is a legitimate concern of God's stewards to be interested in the care of the natural world.

11. Is the natural world included in the apocalyptic hope?

12. Describe biblical stewardship in your own words.

[The following additional materials on tithing and related topics have been produced by GC Church Ministries during 1991-1994: *Life Principles, SDA Financial Systems, Tithing Moments, Stewardship and Strategic Planning.*]

Endnotes

1. Langdon Gilkey, *Maker of Heaven and Earth* (Garden City, NY: Doubleday, 1959), p 83.
2. C J Labuschagne, *The Incomparability of Yahweh in the Old Testament* (Leiden: E J Brill, 1966), p 74. We should point out that in the Old Testament "the dominating characteristic causing Yahweh to be incomparable is His miraculous intervention in history as the redeeming God" (ibid, p 91). However, His activity as Creator is another factor (ibid, pp 108, 109); cf Isaiah 40:18, 25.
3. Hans-Joachim Kraus, *Psalms 1-59: A Commentary* (Minneapolis: Augsburgh, 1988), p 313.
4. J P Baker, "Love," in *New Dictionary of Theology*, S B Ferguson; D F Wright; and J I Packer, eds (Downers Grove, IL: InterVarsity Press, 1988), p 399.
5. See A Nygren, *Agape and Eros* (Philadelphia: Westminster, 1958), p 77.
6. On love within the Godhead consult H W Hoehner, "Love," in *Evangelical Dictionary of Theology*, Walter A Alwell, ed. (Grand Rapids, MI: Baker, 1984), p 657.
7. This line of reasoning was originated by Augustine; see Karl Burger, "Love," in *The New Schaff-Herzog Encyclopedia of Religious Knowledge*, S M Jackson, ed (Grand Rapids, MI: Baker, reprint 1977), vol 7, p 49.
8. E G White, *Testimonies*, vol 5, p 739.
9. For an excellent discussion on the biblical doctrine of man and the meaning of God's image, consult G C Berkouwer, *Man: The Image of God* (Grand Rapids, MI: Eerdmans, 1962), pp 67-118. Among the Adventist scholars who have addressed this subject are V N Olsen, *Man, the Image of God* (Hagerstown, MD: Review and Herald, 1988); and M Veloso, *El Hombre: Una Persona Viviente* (Santiago de Urile: Editorial Universitaria, 1990), pp 79-89.
10. E G White, *The Great Controversy* (Mountain View, CA: Pacific Press, 1911), pp 644, 645.
11. See John A T Robinson, *The Body* (London: SCM Press, 1952), p 14.
12. See K Barth, *Church Dogmatics: The Doctrine of Creation*, vol 3:1 (Edinburg: T & T Clark, 1958), pp 195-201.
13. E G White, *Education*, p 17.
14. See D Jobling, "Dominion Over Creation," in *The Interpreter's Dictionary of the Bible*: Supplementary Volume, K Creim, ed (Nashville, TN: Abingdon, 1976), p 247.
15. See H W Wolff, *Anthropology of the Old Testament* (Philadelphia: Fortress, 1974), p 163.
16. G J Wenham, *Genesis 1-15* (Waco, TX: Word, 1987), p 33.
17. Cf Jobling, "Dominion," p 247.
18. W Brueggemann, *Genesis* (Atlanta: John Knox, 1982), p 32.
19. E G White, *Patriarchs and Prophets*, p 45.
20. Cf Wolff, *Anthropology*, p 162.
21. Ibid.
22. Claus Westermann, *Genesis 1-11: A Commentary* (Minneapolis: Augsburgh, 1984), p 224, writes: "The prohibition which restricts the man hems him in with threat. The limitation is expressed in the law, and here in the sentence, `In the

day that you eat of it you shall die.' This is not in fact a threat of death, but rather the clear expression of the limit which is the necessary accompaniment of the freedom entrusted to humanity in the command. To say no to God—and this is what freedom allows—is ultimately to say no to life; for life comes from God."

23. E G White, *Patriarchs and Prophets*, p 53.
24. For a discussion of the different options, see Westermann, Genesis 1-11, pp 242-248.
25. Victor P Hamilton, *The Book of Genesis: Chapters 1-17* (Grand Rapids, MI: Eerdmans, 1990), p 166, writes, "What is forbidden to man is the power to decide for himself what is in his best interest and what is not. This is a decision God has not delegated to the earthling."
26. E G White, "E G White Comments: Romans," in *SDA Bible Commentary*, vol 6, p 1078.
27. E G White, *Testimonies*, vol 4, p 294.
28. E G White, *Ministry of Healing*, p 163.
29. Cf Peter Pokorny, *Colossians: A Commentary* (Peabody, MA: Hendrickson, 1991), p 74.
30. See Eduard Lohse, *Colossians and Philemon* (Philadelphia: Fortress, 1971), pp 48, 49.
31. See Rudolf Schnackenburg, *The Gospel According to John*, vol 1 (New York: Seabury Press, 1968), p 388.
32. Arthur Patzia, *Ephesians, Colossians, Philemon* (Peabody, MA: Hendrickson, 1984), p 155. Marcus Barth, Ephesians 1-3 (Garden City, NY: Doubleday, 1974), p 76, translates the first part of Ephesians 1:10 as, "that he should administer the days of fulfillment." According to him, Christ is described in that verse as a steward of God (pp 86-89).
33. M Lattke, "Keno_ make empty, destroy," in *Exegetical Dictionary of the New Testament*, vol 2, Horst Balz and Gerhard Schneider, eds (Grand Rapids, MI: Eerdmans, 1991), p 282, wrote concerning Christ in 2 Cor 8:9, "that the clause speaks of the self-giving humility and self-denying impoverishment of the divine manner of being."
34. See Ángel Manuel Rodríguez, "Salvation by Sacrificial Substitution," *Journal of the Adventist Theological Society*, vol 3 (1992), pp 65-68.
35. C E B Cranfield, The Epistle to the Romans, vol 1 (Edinburgh: T & T Clark, 1975), p 432.
36. H Balz, "Mataiotēs vanity, nothingness, transitoriness," in *Exegetical Dictionary of the New Testament*, vol 2, p 397. For a discussion of the close connection between humans and nature according to the Bible and its significance for modern society, see Frank Moore Cross, "The Redemption of Nature," Princeton Seminary Bulletin, vol 10 (1989), pp 94-104.

STEWARDSHIP AND THE THEOLOGY OF TITHE

Introduction

This study will examine the biblical evidence that describes the tithing system, in an attempt to explore its essential characteristics and theological content. Biblical scholars have shown little interest in the study of the Israelite tithing system. Most studies on this subject have been controlled by historical, critical concerns (reconstructing the historical development of the system and dating the different sources) rather than by theological interest.[1] We would rather approach the text in its canonical form, paying particular attention to its theological motivation.

It is a well-known fact that tithing is not an exclusively Israelite practice. Records, for instance, from the city of Ugarit (14th century BC) indicate that its residents paid tithe to the temple, a kind of tax, and that the king also received a royal tax (a tithe) from the people.[2]

Neo-Babylonian documents from the 6th century BC reveal that tithing was a common practice in Babylon. The tithe was given to the temple, and the king himself was expected to tithe. Tithe was collected from all goods, including barley, dates, sesame, flax, oil, garlic, wool, clothes, cattle, sheep, birds, wood, and products of silver and gold.[3] Tithing was also known and practiced among Persians, Greeks, and Romans.[4]

The origin of this widespread practice is unknown to historians. The Bible does not discuss it, and when tithing is mentioned for the first time, it seems to have been already a common practice.

Nevertheless, we do know that "the tithing system reaches back beyond the days of Moses. . . . Even as far back as the days of Adam."[5] The system, as revealed in the Old Testament, is "divine in its origin";[6] it was given by God to man. Tithing seems to be associated with humankind in its fallen state.

As follows, we will examine the biblical passages in which tithing is discussed or mentioned. We will emphasize the theological ideas associated with it and its purpose. Then we will integrate those ideas and concepts to provide a broad picture of the biblical understanding of tithing.

Tithing in the Old Testament

Genesis 14: Abraham's Tithe

Genesis 14 is a unique chapter in the patriarchal history that allows us to become acquainted with an important aspect of Abraham's life as a military leader. Among his servants was a well-trained group of soldiers.

Yet, the purpose of Genesis 14 is not just to describe Abraham's leadership abilities in time of war, but to reveal a more important dimension of his character and the characters of those mentioned in the narrative. Through their actions and attitudes, the purposes and motivations of their hearts were revealed, and we are able to perceive a marked contrast between Abraham and Melchizedek on the one hand, and the kings on the other hand.

The differences between those two groups were determined by their commitment or lack of commitment to the Lord Most High. Those who did not serve Him are depicted as covetous and self-centered, totally possessed and controlled by their selfish hearts, recognizing no other authority than their own. There was no place in their hearts for gratitude, and much less for recognition of their limitations as creatures of the Lord.

Abraham and Melchizedek exhibit a very unselfish spirit in the narrative. Both have an important thing in common: they worship the Lord Most High and recognize Him as the Creator of heaven and earth. It is within this theological setting that tithing is introduced in the story.

Genesis 14 deals with properties, and the loss and recovery of goods. The cities of the plain had been under the political control of Kedarlaomer for twelve years. His expansionistic policies and his desire for power led him to conquer those cities, forcing the people to pay him high annual taxes. By dispossessing others of their goods, the king was enriching himself and feeding his selfish heart in the process.

After twelve years of oppression, the inhabitants of the cities decided to rebel but were easily defeated. King Kedarlaomer and his allies attacked and subdued them, and took food and goods from the king of Sodom and from Lot. Some of the people, including Lot, were taken prisoner.

Abraham was informed about these events and decided to intervene to liberate Lot. He attacked and defeated the kings, setting the prisoners free and recovering all the goods taken from Lot and the king of Sodom. As he was returning, the kings of Sodom and Salem came out to meet him. Abraham gave the tithe of the spoils to Melchizedek, and gave the king of Sodom everything that had been taken from him.

The practice of tithing is mentioned here in an almost casual way, suggesting that tithing was already part of Abraham's religious life and experience. This was certainly not the first time he had returned his tithe to the servant of God. As we read the story, we realize that several important elements concerning the practice of tithing are brought into focus:

Tithe Is Based on Income

Having defeated the enemy, the spoils of war belonged to Abraham, including what was taken from Lot, the king of Sodom, and the prisoners. Abraham could have come out of this experience greatly enriched. However, his decision to go to war had not been motivated by selfish concern but rather by a desire to save Lot.

Abraham's unselfishness is manifested in the narrative in two ways. First, he gave back to the king of Sodom what Kedarlaomer had taken from him. Before Abraham went to war, he had promised God that if he was successful, he would return everything to the king of Sodom, because he was not interested in direct or indirect personal benefit from this experience.

Second, Abraham demonstrated his unselfishness by giving a tithe of everything to the king of Salem. The passage states clearly that he "gave tithe of every thing" (14:20). It is rather difficult to know what is included in that phrase. Probably, it would be right to conclude that he did not tithe the goods of the king of Sodom. Apparently, he never considered those to be his. If that was the case, he returned tithe on the spoils of war that he considered to be his. This was new income for him. Notice that the verb used is "give" (*nathan*). The tithe was not his, and he returned it to the Lord.

The Recipient of Tithe

The narrative reveals who should receive the tithe. Melchizedek was not only a king, but also priest of the Lord. He and Abraham worshipped the Lord Most High (identified as Yahweh by Abraham). There were some among the Canaanites who still worshipped the true God, and Melchizedek was one of them.

As Abraham was returning victoriously from the conflict, Melchizedek went to welcome and provide for him. He prepared a royal banquet for Abraham. In addition, he blessed Abraham. Melchizedek had been chosen by God to function as a priest and be the mediator of God's blessing. Immediately after the blessing Abraham gave him the tithe. It was in his role as priest that Melchizedek received the tithe, and on that same basis Abraham gave it to him.

Tithe is returned to an instrument appointed by God to serve Him and His people as priest. By giving the tithe to this priest, Abraham implicitly recognized the sanctity of tithe. It was returned to the one selected by God to be His holy instrument. Only he could handle holy things.

Theological Basis for Tithing

The narrative provides certain theological concepts that shed some light on the meaning of tithing. These concepts, which underlie the practice of tithing, suggest that tithing is not an isolated phenomenon in a person's religious experience, but that it belongs to a particular theological understanding of the world around us and of our role within it.

A. God Is the Creator: This idea is so important that it is mentioned twice in the narrative. Melchizedek and Abraham refer to God as the "creator of heaven and earth." The God invoked in the blessing is the Creator.

The Hebrew word translated "Creator" (*qanah*) comes from a root that means "to acquire, possess (stressing possessing)." One can possess something by making, creating, or acquiring it. In this narrative, the term *qanah* seems to express the ideas of creation and possession. Everything in heaven and on earth belongs to the Lord because He created it. God's ownership is based on His activity as Creator.

This suggests that ultimate reality is unity; we are not expected to answer to different spiritual powers, only to the Creator. Our loyalty is not to be divided between different lords, because there is only one Lord who brought into existence everything that is.

Without the biblical concept of creation, tithing lacks solid meaning. Abraham tithed because his God was the Creator of heaven and earth. He recognized God's ownership through the confession of his mouth, "Lord, God Most High, Creator of heaven and earth" (Genesis 14:22,), and through his actions by returning the tithe to Melchizedek.

B. God Is the One Who Blesses: As we pointed out, Melchizedek fulfilled a priestly responsibility by blessing Abraham. Theologically, blessing precedes tithing. Without this prior blessing, true tithing is impossible.

God's blessings are always an expression of His love and concern for us. Tithing is a recognition of the Lord's goodness, and, therefore, it is always a response and never a prelude.

Abraham was fully aware of the fact that the one who enriched him was the Lord. He was persuaded in his own mind that his financial security was not dependent upon anyone's power, but upon God's blessings. When the king of Sodom said to him (in an almost demanding tone), "give me the people and keep the goods," Abraham's reaction was immediate, "I will accept nothing." (See Genesis 14:21 23.) Melchizedek went out to meet Abraham to share food and a blessing; the king of Sodom went to demand that at least part of his properties be returned to him. Technically, the king of Sodom's goods belonged to Abraham. But Abraham gave back everything to him for two reasons. We have already stated the first one: Abraham pronounced an oath before the Lord committing himself to return everything that belonged to the king. Second, Abraham did not want the king to say, "I enriched Abraham." In this way, Abraham was protecting God's honor.

The patriarch knew that his wealth was the result of God's blessings, and he was not willing to allow anyone to weaken or distort that conviction. He rejected wealth rather than cast a shadow on God's goodness by receiving it. The implication is that Abraham's primary concern was not his own material or economic well-being, but his relationship with the Lord. That was where his willingness to tithe originated.

C. God Preserves Human Life: The narrative suggests that tithing is theologically motivated. In this specific case, Abraham's tithe was "a recognition that it was God Most High who had given him the victory" (verse 20).[7] The priest, in the blessing, praised God because He defeated the enemies by giving them into Abraham's hands. The role of Abraham is not denied, but the victory is ascribed to God.

Tithing was based not only on the fact that God blessed Abraham, but also on the fact that He preserved him by defeating the enemies. The implication is that life is so fragile that it cannot be fully preserved by human efforts. There are forces that threaten human life, and only God can properly and effectively defeat them. This conviction was so dynamic that it embodied itself in Abraham's act of tithing. Hence, tithing expresses the fact that life is not ours but always belongs to the Lord (not just because He created us, but because He preserves us in a world of sin and death).

According to Genesis 14, tithing is a rejection of selfishness. This enslaving power rules over those who are not acquainted with the Lord, and leads them to exploit and destroy others in their pursuit of wealth. Abraham tithed because he had rejected selfishness as the force that ruled his life.

At a deeper level, Abraham's tithing practice was based on the solid conviction that God is the Creator and Owner of everything in the universe—the One who blesses and preserves life. Abraham's experience makes clear that the Lord has chosen specific individuals to mediate the transfer of tithe from the worshiper to Him. A priest received it in this particular case, and in other cases recorded in the Old Testament. Abraham returned his tithe to one of God's appointed instruments.

Genesis 28:10-22: Jacob's Tithe

The second reference to tithing in the Bible is found in Genesis 28:22, where we read that Jacob left home and headed toward Haran to preserve his life. Between Beersheba and Haran he had an experience with the Lord that sustained him throughout the remainder of his life.

The Lord appeared to Jacob in a dream, revealing Himself as a loving and caring God willing to bless, guide, and protect the patriarch. In response to this divine revelation, Jacob made a vow promising to return a tithe on everything God gave him.

The context of this commitment to tithing provides basic and meaningful concepts that will assist us in uncovering a number of theological ideas associated with tithing.

Jacob's Commitment to God

Just before Jacob promised to tithe, he said, "then the Lord will be my God" (28:21). During the dream, the Lord promised to give Jacob a number of things because of His gracious love. The Lord revealed Himself as the God of Abraham and Isaac, but His real intent was to become Jacob's God also (verse 13). But that was Jacob's decision to make, and he decided in favor of God.

Commitment to the Lord in a relationship of love precedes tithing because tithe is inseparably connected to the Lord; it belongs to Him. Tithe is based on a recognition of God's providential intervention in the life of a person. Without that prior experience and commitment, tithing lacks purpose and becomes irrelevant or meaningless.

God's Concern for Jacob

In the dream, God described Himself as the One who would provide for Jacob's needs. The specific promises revealed in a particular way what the Lord was going to give the patriarch.

A. Descendants (see Genesis 28:14): Jacob traveled alone, but that would change in the future. His descendants, the Lord said, "will be like the dust of the earth." Through him, the promises made to Abraham would be fulfilled. The implication was that human procreation is in the hands of the Lord, not under the control of the law of human reproduction.

B. Protection (see Genesis 28:15): The promise of protection implied that Jacob lived in a hostile environment and that alone, he was unable to preserve himself. He was promised what he needed: divine guidance. Thus is emphasized the limits of human power and the need to rely on a greater-than-human power. The preservation of life is ultimately in the hands of the Lord.

C. Land (see Genesis 28:13): The land was one of the most important gifts the Lord gave His people. Land provided them with an identity and was, to a large extent, a source of wealth and financial security. This promise implied that the land belonged to the Lord, not to the people, and it was God who provided financial security.

D. Goods (see Genesis 28:20): God promised Jacob that He would provide bread and clothes for him. This must have brought peace of mind to the lonely traveler.

Through these promises, the Lord revealed Himself to Jacob as the One who is the very center of human security, the supreme and only source of true blessings. He possesses everything and apportions it to every person according to His loving will. God is the Owner, but He has a natural disposition to share with others. Notice how this idea is stressed in the way the promises are phrased: the Lord is always the subject.

> "I will give to you the land."
> "I am with you."
> "I will watch over you."
> "I will bring you back to this land."
> "I will not abandon you."
> "I will do what I have promised."

God described Himself here as the One who possessed the power Jacob needed to realize himself, to become what he should become. This was the power of God's loving presence in his life.

Then Jacob said, "Of all that you give me, I will give you a tenth" (28:22). He realized that whatever he obtained in the future would always be a gift from God. He would never possess anything except what the Lord gave him. For him, tithe would be an expression of gratitude, a recognition that he did not own anything.

Jacob Makes a Vow

A vow was a very solemn act by which one determined to take God seriously, committing oneself to His word. It was a way of expressing faith in the Lord. In his vow, Jacob did not negotiate with God or attempt to bribe Him. "The Lord had already promised him prosperity, and this vow was the outflow of a heart filled with gratitude for the assurance of God's love and mercy."[8]

Through the vow, Jacob appropriated God's promises. In fact, his "vow matches the promises."[9] Everything the patriarch mentions in his vow—God's protective care, food and clothes, his return safely to the land—God already promised him. We are right in concluding that, through the vow, Jacob was taking God seriously and accepting His gracious offer.

Tithing is part of the vow. But if tithe belongs to the Lord, then why make a vow promising to return it to Him? Several reasons can be given:

A. Tithe and the Vow: By making a vow Jacob recognized that tithe belongs to the Lord. Otherwise, he may have been tempted to simply consider it part of his income and return it to God whenever he felt like it. In a sense, this vow was a witness to the sanctity of tithe.

B. Voluntary Nature of Tithe: By making a vow Jacob expressed his free-will decision to return the tithe to the Lord. God had not forced him to tithe. Vows in the Bible always are voluntary acts based on the working of the Spirit on the heart of the individual. Jacob's vow meant that he had chosen voluntarily to return to the Lord what was His.

C. Trust in God: By making a vow, Jacob accepted God's challenge to trust in Him or to test Him (cf Malachi 3:10.) God made specific promises to Jacob hoping that he would accept and believe them. This required from Jacob an entering into a relationship of trust and confidence in the Lord.

A vow is a most solemn act by which a person expresses confidence in the Lord. In a sense it is faith growing into maturity. In the case of Jacob, tithing was a part of his full commitment in faith to the Lord. His vow makes clear that God's blessings precede tithing, and that, therefore, tithing is not a way of gaining God's favor.

Jacob Worshipped

Tithe is mentioned in this story in a context of worship. Jacob was confronted by God's beaming presence, and he worshiped. That is what worship is—a reverent response to God's presence. The place where he had the dream became a place of worship, a house of the Lord. Tithing is one element in the act of worship.

A reading of verses 21 and 22 of chapter 28 indicates that Jacob's vow included three basic components: (1) commitment to the Lord ("the Lord will be my God"); (2) worshiping Him (the place became "a cultic center"); (3) tithing (based on what God gave him). Tithing is meaningful only within that theological setting.

A most important element in this narrative is the fact that tithing is preceded by a revelation of God as a caring and loving Person, always willing to bless and preserve the life of His servant. Jacob discovered that every spiritual and material blessing is found in the Lord and that He has a natural disposition to bless abundantly.

According to this narrative, it is probably correct to conclude that tithing is based on an ethics of imitation. God is the Great Giver, and Jacob imitated Him when he tithed. In a sense this is similar to the Sabbath commandment. Resting on the Sabbath is based on the fact that God rested on that day. In fulfilling the commandment, we imitate Him.

Such imitational ethics become a possibility only after the person accepts God as His personal Lord. It encompasses a full surrender of the individual's life and possessions to the Lord. Tithing perpetuates that experience in the life of the person. If a vow is involved, it is because the relationship with the Lord is a formal one and the commitment is permanent. As an act of worship, tithing renews our constant willingness to surrender our life to the Source of all blessings, reaffirming our unconditional commitment to God. In that sense, tithe is a concrete representation of covenant.

Tithing Legislation

The Lord incorporated tithing into the Israelite covenant law, making it part of the people's religious experience as a nation. Several laws in the Pentateuch address tithing practices. The intent of those regulations is to define what should be tithed, to explain the process to be followed when tithing, to define the use of tithe, and to state the theological and social function of tithe. We proceed to examine that legislation.

Leviticus 27:30-33

Leviticus 27 deals with dedicatory gifts—that is, gifts promised to the Lord through a vow or by consecrating them to Him. These gifts include votive offerings of persons in fixed amounts of silver (verses 1-8); pledges of animals (verses 9-13); consecration of property or land (verses 14 24); and ban laws (verses 28, 29). The chapter also includes laws regulating the redemption of firstborn and tithe (verses

26, 27; 30-33).[10]

The basic purpose of the chapter is to define the main sources of income for the sanctuary services and the priests.[11] Funding the sanctuary was an extremely important part of the Israelite system of worship, because through it the people showed their joy and gratitude for having God dwelling among them.

Although tithing was not a voluntary offering, it was included among the dedicatory offerings because it was also a source of income for the clergy. Besides, dedicatory offerings were redeemable, and, to a certain extent, so was the tithe. Therefore, it was quite logical to include tithe in the discussion of dedicatory offerings. This specific legislation of tithing states some significant facts.

A. Tithing Is Based on a Theological Conviction: Tithe belongs to the Lord and therefore is holy. It does not become holy through a vow or a consecration act. It is simply holy by its very nature; it belongs to the Lord. No one except God has a right to it. No one can consecrate it to the Lord, because tithe is never part of a person's property.

In a sense, tithe is like the Sabbath. Both are holy to the Lord (qodesh laYHWH; Exodus 16:23; Leviticus 27:30). God invested them with holiness, and now it is part of their very nature. Both can become a test of loyalty to the Lord and to the covenant, because the Lord put them at our disposal even though neither of the two is ours. We can desecrate both of them by using them in a profane way.

B. Tithe Is Based on the Increase of Goods: The legislation requires tithing all the produce of the earth: grains and fruits. It also applies to the increase of "herds and flocks." The literal translation of that phrase is "ox and sheep," but in Leviticus it designates "herds and flocks" (Leviticus 1:10).[12] This increase in produce and livestock is the result of God's blessings on His people (Leviticus 26:3-5). Tithing is a recognition on the part of Israel that everything they have comes from and belongs to the Lord. This recognition lies at the very heart of the covenant. Tithing becomes a constant witness to the covenant and to the people's loyalty to it.[13]

C. Redemption of Tithe: Tithe from the yield of the field can be redeemed by substituting it with an equivalent, (probably in silver), plus a surcharge of twenty percent. Tithe from herds and flocks was not redeemable.

The redemption of tithe mentioned here should not be confused with the erroneous practice of withholding tithe with the intention of bringing it later and adding twenty percent to it. What this legislation establishes is that since tithe is paid in kind, "there might be cases in which a man needed wheat for sowing, and would rather pay in money than in wheat. Under these conditions, he might redeem the tithe by having the wheat appraised and paying this sum plus one fifth."[14] There is no indication in Leviticus 27 that tithe may be withheld.

D. Tithe Is Not to be Manipulated: The person is commanded to bring the tithe to the Lord. Any attempt to manipulate the system in an effort to obtain some personal gain is rejected by this legislation.

The Israelites were not to control or influence in any way the selection of tithe from the herds and flocks. Every tenth animal that passed under the shepherd's rod belonged to the Lord. The person was not to "pick out the good from the bad or make any substitution" (Leviticus 27:33). The quality of the animal was not to be controlled at all.

Leviticus 27 defines tithe as holy to the Lord. It also associates tithing with gifts given to the sanctuary in order to fund it and its clergy. That is probably one of the reasons for redeeming it; through redemption, cash (silver) was provided to the sanctuary. This legislation does not state clearly how tithe was to be used in the sanctuary. The emphasis is on the nature of tithe and the responsibility of the individual to bring it to the Lord.

Numbers 18:21-32

Numbers 18 describes the responsibility of priests and Levites as guardians of the sanctuary. Guarding the sanctuary and ministering to the needs of the people was a full-time job. The tribe of Levi had no inheritance among the rest of Israel; the Lord was their inheritance. God was the One who provided for their needs. The main purpose of Numbers 18 is to address "the means by which the clerical orders . . . are to be maintained."[15]

The Lord assigned the gifts the people brought to Him to Aaron. These included a portion of the most holy (verses 9, 10) and holy offerings (verses 11-19). He also benefited from the tithe (verses 25-32).[16]

The income of the Levites was the tithe returned by the Israelites to the Lord (verses 21-24). Tithe is discussed here in the context of the sanctuary and is directly related to the work of priests and Levites.

A. Nature of Tithe: Numbers 18 does not refer to tithe explicitly as a gift holy to the Lord. Tithe is probably included in the phrase "the holy offerings of the Israelites" (verse 32), or perhaps it refers exclusively to tithe, but that is not absolutely certain.

Nevertheless, tithe is described as that which "the Israelites present as an offering to the Lord" (verse 24). The verb translated "present" (*rûm*) means "set apart (picked out and), present." "An offering" (*terûmah*) seems to refer to something that is designated (set apart) as an offering outside the sanctuary and subsequently brought to the sanctuary and offered to the Lord.[17] If that interpretation is right, then tithe was an offering set apart at home and later returned to the Lord at the sanctuary.

By describing tithe as an offering, its holiness is being indicated. The fact that it is an offering does not mean that it was a voluntary one; the Lord did require it from the people.[18] This legislation does not define what should be tithed. There is an incidental mention of "grain" and "wine" (verse 27), but the text does not limit tithing only to those items (see verses 28, 29.)

B. Use of Tithe: Tithe belongs to the Lord, but He assigned it to the Levites (verse 21). This decision was based on the fact that the Levites did not receive any inheritance among the Israelites and consequently did not have a way of sustenance. Their function was to minister in the sanctuary and to protect its holiness. The Lord gave them the tithe as compensation (verse 21; *heleph*) or a reward (verse 31; *sakar*) for their work in the sanctuary.

Notice that in tithing, the Israelites were not paying the Levites for their services. They were only returning the tithe to the Lord in the form of an offering. It was the Lord who decided how to use it. The Lord decided to give it to the Levites.

The significance of this procedure is found in the fact that the quality of the services rendered by the Levites to the Israelites did not affect the tithing practice of the people at all. They returned their tithe to the Lord, and He gave it to the Levites. That idea is repeated three times in the chapter (verses 21, 24, 25).

This same approach was also used concerning the tithe assigned to the priests (verses 28, 29). The Levites were commanded to present a tithe from the tithe returned to the Lord, but it was the Lord who determined how it was to be used. The tithe of the Levites was for the Lord, and was not a payment made to the priests for their services: "You must present a tenth of that tithe as the Lord's offering" (verse 25). The sustenance of the priests was not in the hands of the Levites, but of the Lord. This tithe was selected from the best portion of the tithe of the Israelites (verse 29), thereby avoiding any attempt on the part of the Levites to manipulate the process.

According to Numbers 18 then, tithe was assigned by the Lord to the Levites and priests as compensation for their full time work in the sanctuary on behalf of the people of Israel. Tithe was brought to the Lord, and was not payment for the ministry of Levites and priests. In fact, tithe never appears as payment for services received.

Deuteronomy 12:6, 11, 17; 14:22-29; 26:12-15

Deuteronomy 12 deals with the importance of worshiping God at one central sanctuary—a place chosen by the Lord. To this place the Israelites were expected to bring their sacrifices, offerings, and tithe (verses 6, 11).

In 12:17 we find instructions related to the use of tithe that we do not find in other legislation. The Israelites were commanded not to eat the tithe in their own towns but to take it to the central sanctuary. They ate it in the presence of the Lord (verse 18). The whole household was allowed to eat.

The legislation recorded in 14:22-27 further developed those ideas. Deuteronomy 14 deals with "that which may or may not be eaten."[19] The tithe of grain, new wine, and oil is mentioned among the foods that could be eaten (verses 22, 23). The Israelites were required to take this tithe to the sanctuary and eat it in the presence of the Lord.

If the central sanctuary was too distant, the people were allowed to exchange the tithe for silver. Once they reached the sanctuary, they bought whatever they liked with the silver. "You and your household shall eat it there in the presence of the Lord and rejoice" (verse 26). In doing this, they were not to neglect the Levites—they were to share the food with them.

It is obvious that there are significant differences between this legislation and that found in Leviticus and Numbers. The most important differences are:

A. Objects of Tithe: In Deuteronomy tithe was imposed only on grain, wine, and oil, while in the other legislation all the produce of the earth and the increase of herds and flocks were to be tithed.

B. Levitical Tithe: Although the tithe discussed in Deuteronomy was required by the Lord, it belonged to the family that brought it to the sanctuary. Leviticus and Numbers deal with a tithe that belonged exclusively to God, and that was given by Him to the Levites and priests.

C. Fellowship Meals: Tithe in Deuteronomy was to be used by the Israelites for a family fellowship meal to be eaten at the central sanctuary. The other legislations did not allow for that. They limited the eating of the tithe to the Levites, the priests, and their respective families.

The conclusion seems inescapable that we are dealing here with two different types of tithe. It does not seem possible to parallel what we have in Deuteronomy with the legislation in Leviticus and Numbers.[20] Rabbinic traditions called the tithe recorded in Leviticus "the first tithe," and the one in Deuteronomy "the second tithe."

To complicate matters even further, Deuteronomy 14:28, 29, and 26:12-15 mention a tithe that was to be given in the third year. This tithe was from the produce of the earth and was supposed to be kept in the towns. Its purpose was that "the Levites . . . and the aliens, the fatherless and the widows who live in your towns may come and eat and be satisfied" (14:29).

Is this a third tithe? Some have interpreted it as a third tithe, but others have argued that this legislation describes a different use of the second tithe every three years. This last interpretation is probably right. For two years the second tithe was brought to the sanctuary and eaten there by the Israelites, but "every third year . . . this second tithe was to be used at home, in entertaining the Levites and the poor."[21]

This second tithe was also based on the conviction that it was God who blessed Israel (12:6, 7). However, its purpose was to teach reverence to the Lord (14:22) and to provide for the needy (26:12). This tithe seems to have been a "charity" tithe within the Israelite theocracy.

Other Old Testament Passages

There are a few other places in the Old Testament where tithe is mentioned. We will examine them to explore their contribution to the nature and theology of tithing.

2 Chronicles 31:4-6, 12

Tithe is mentioned here in the context of the religious reform promulgated by Hezekiah. Under his leadership the temple was cleansed and rededicated (2 Chronicles 29), the passover was celebrated (2 Chronicles 30), and he appealed to the people to provide for priests and Levites by bringing their first fruits and tithes to the temple (2 Chronicles 31). Under Ahaz, the previous king of Judah, the doors of the temple were closed, bringing an end to the worship services. In that national apostasy, the people stopped bringing their tithe to the temple.

What Chronicles 31 states about tithing is brief and in agreement with what we found in Leviticus and Numbers.

A. Objects Tithed: Tithe was solicited from all the produce of the earth and from the increase of herds and flocks (verses 5, 6).

B. Tithe Called an Offering: Tithe was described as, or called, an "offering" (terûmah). This is the same term used in Numbers to refer to tithe and suggests that tithe is returned to the Lord.

C. The Purpose of Tithe: Tithe was used to provide for the needs of Levites and priests in order for them to "devote themselves to the Law of the Lord" (verse 4).

D. Everything a Gift From God: Tithing was preceded by God's blessings and, therefore, recognized that all that the people had was given to them by the Lord (verse 10).

Possibly, the new element concerning tithe in this narrative is provided by its context.

Apostasy leads almost inexorably to a rejection of tithing. Ahaz concluded that the one who blessed him was not the Lord but the gods of Aram (2 Chronicles 28:23), consequently, he and the people of Judah stopped bringing their tithes to the Lord.

Amos 4:4

There were two cultic centers in the northern kingdom—one was in Bethel, the other in Gilgal. Undoubtedly, these were centers of idolatry, but in his sermons Amos's primarily attacked the sin of religious formalism—the performance of religious acts at those centers that had no practical impact on the life of the individual. The people and their leaders had separated religious concerns from morality and justice.

Amos described the people's religious zeal as sinful, and sarcastically invited them to continue to perform their rituals in order to increase their sinfulness: "Go to Bethel and sin; go to Gilgal and sin yet more. Bring your sacrifices every morning, your tithe every three days."[22]

Amos declared that the more the people "attend the cultic sites and the more zealous they are in performing the manyfold attendant rites, the more they continue to offend and transgress."[23] Religion without ethics, morality, and justice is an act of rebellion against the Lord. The "substitution of cultic offerings for justice toward the oppressed" is a sinful act.[24] Religious zeal is not necessarily a manifestation of true piety.

Amos said that tithe becomes meaningless if it is not accompanied by a religious experience that has a major impact on the person's social behavior and concern for others. A formal or legalistic religious life robs tithing of its intrinsic meaning.

Nehemiah 10:38,39; 12:44; 13:5, 12

Nehemiah 10:38,39 forms part of a covenant renewal ceremony. The small community of Jews who returned to Jerusalem met together with the leaders to read the Law of Moses (Nehemiah 8), to confess their sins (Nehemiah 9), and to renew the covenant with the Lord (Nehemiah 10). Tithing is mentioned among the covenant stipulations. During the ceremony, the Jews committed themselves to bringing their tithe to the Lord. The Levites, accompanied by priests, went to the towns to collect the tithe from the people and take at least some of it to the temple's storerooms.[25]

This legislation closely follows the instruction found in Numbers. The tithe was for the Levites, but they gave a tenth of it to the priests (10:38). It is specifically stated that a tithe was collected from the crops (verse 39), but that did not necessarily exclude a tithe from the increase of herds and flocks, since the people wanted to do what was "required by the law" (12:44).

The reference to tithe in 10:38, 39, is followed by the people's commitment to the preservation of the temple's services: "We will not neglect the house of our God" (verse 39). By giving their tithe, they showed their concern for the temple, which was God's dwelling place. They wanted to continue to benefit from God's gracious forgiveness through the intercessory ministry of the priests.

Later, Nehemiah appointed a group of Levites to be in charge of the storerooms in the temple. They collected the tithe from the towns (Nehemiah 12:44). The system set up by Nehemiah was functional and gained the support of the Jews.

It is at this point in the narrative that an important detail is added: "Judah was pleased with the ministering priests and Levites" (verse 44). Notice that the people's reason for tithing was *not* that they were pleased with the performance of the priests. They tithed because, according to the law, that was what the Lord expected from them. They, as well as the priests and Levites, were fulfilling God's will and the result was joy in the Lord. Of course, this does not mean that the Jews were not interested in what was going on in the temple.

After twelve years in Jerusalem, Nehemiah returned to Persia (ca. 432 BC). Soon after his departure, the spiritual condition of the people began to deteriorate. The priests lost sight of their high calling. Eliashib, the priest in charge of the storerooms for the tithe, allowed Tobiah, an Ammonite, to take up residence in one of the storerooms inside the temple, thereby profaning it (13:4, 5). At that time, the Sabbath was not kept properly (13:15); the people stopped giving tithe (13:10); and the Levites left their post at the temple and went to work in the fields (13:10).

Nehemiah returned unexpectedly to Jerusalem and became aware of the spiritual fall of the people and their leaders. His first act was to oust Tobiah from the temple and to reconsecrate the place. Next he called the Levites back to the temple and asked the people to bring their tithes to the Lord.

The failure of the people to bring their tithes to the Lord was influenced by what was taking place in the temple under the leadership of the priests.[26] The fact that the temple was profaned and that the offerings were being misused "tended to discourage the liberalities of the people. They had lost their zeal and fervor, and were reluctant to pay their tithes. The treasuries of the Lord's house were poorly supplied."[27] Nehemiah's reforms "inspired the people with confidence and all of Judah brought the tithes" to the Lord.[28]

Was the attitude of the people right? Was it justifiable for them to retain the tithe or stop tithing because of the corruption among the priests? Certainly not. Nehemiah did not condone the attitude of the people but reminded them of their commitment to the temple (10:39).

He called in the "officials," or leaders of the people. These were not from the priesthood. The term "officials" (*seganim*) designated "minor officials, such as village leaders."[29] In addressing and rebuking these leaders who represented the people, Nehemiah was rebuking the people for not returning their tithes to the house of the Lord. The Hebrew verb translated "to rebuke" is a very strong legal term (*rîb*). It means "to dispute, quarrel (in public, with words, complaints, assertions, reproaches)."[30] The Lord expected both the priests and the people to fulfill their respective responsibilities.[31]

This failure on the part of the priests and Levites had to be corrected. Nehemiah selected four trustworthy men to be in charge of the storerooms who were responsible also "for distributing the supplies to their brothers" (13:13). The reform restored the people's confidence in their leaders.

In the book of Nehemiah, it is pointed out that tithing imposes a responsibility not only on the giver, but also on the receiver. God expects those who administer the tithe to manage it properly. Although improper behavior on the part of those chosen by God to lead His people may discourage the laity, that in no way justifies not returning the tithe to the Lord.

Malachi 3:8-10

In this well-known passage, the refusal to tithe is interpreted as misappropriation of God's property—a robbery. Those in Israel who did not tithe or who gave a partial tithe (the phrase "bring the whole tithe" [verse 10] can be interpreted in both ways), deprived God of what was His.

This accusation was a serious one. Misappropriating what belonged to the Lord was a serious crime in Israel and throughout the ancient Near East. This passage establishes beyond any reasonable doubt that tithe is not part of a person's income. True, it does reach us in the form of income, but it is never ours. To consider it simply as personal income, in order to use it as we wish, is to rob God.

We have seen already that tithe was used by God to provide food for priests and Levites. It is also emphasized here in verse 10. If the people misused tithe, the priests and Levites suffered, but the people's sinful act was committed against the Lord. It was God, not the Levites, who was deprived of what was exclusively His.

At a deeper level, the problem became even more serious. By not bringing their tithes to the Lord, the people made an important religious statement. They denied God's providential and loving care for them. They deprived God of the honor and glory He deserves as the One who preserves them. This lack of faith in the Lord is quoted by Malachi: "You have said, `It is futile to serve God. What did we gain by carrying out His requirements. . . ?'" (3:14). They accused God of not fulfilling His part of the covenant, but the Lord responded, "You are robbing me."

For a people not fully committed to the Lord, tithing is indeed a challenge. They trust only themselves for their own preservation. In this particular situation, the financial condition of the people was precarious, and they considered tithing unnecessary. It was to such individuals that the Lord said, "Test me in this" (verse 10). This was a call to move forward in faith to do what must be done, believing in God's promised blessings (verses 10-12). In the process, the Lord expected their faith to grow to the point of trusting Him absolutely, recognizing that their financial security was found only in Him.

This divine call to faith is meaningless without a conversion experience. The invitation to stop robbing God is introduced by a call to conversion: "Return to me" (verse 7). Genuine tithing is a possibility only for those who return to the Lord in faith—trusting in Him.

To understand even better Malachi's indictment against the Israelites on the matter of tithing, we must put the passage in its historical and religious contexts.

It is generally believed that Malachi prophesied during the time of Ezra and Nehemiah. Since the spiritual condition of the people and their leaders is described in the same way in Malachi and Nehemiah 13, a number of scholars have concluded that Malachi prophesied during the time when Nehemiah went to Persia (ca. 432 BC or shortly thereafter).[32] As we saw, this was a period of great spiritual deterioration in Jerusalem. Malachi described the situation in greater detail than Nehemiah in his two speeches against the priesthood. One is recorded in 1:6-14, the other in 2:1-9.

The first attack against the priesthood is based on their lack of respect for the Lord (1:6). They brought defiled sacrifices to Him; the sacrificial victims were physically defective (1:8) and even sick (1:13). Not even a governor would accept such gifts (verse 8). The priests were also condemned because they considered their work a heavy burden and, therefore, were not following proper procedures (verse 12).

The second passage admonishes the priests to listen to the Lord (2:1). They were not instructing the people properly and had also violated their call to the priesthood (2:7, 8). They preserved, in a corrupt way, an external form of worship.

We are tempted to raise the question, "Do such people deserve to receive the tithe?" But that question was not raised by the prophet. God assigned the priests specific responsibilities, and they were judged on the basis of those responsibilities and on their proper performance. The people were expected to fulfill whatever the Lord commanded them to do, and He did not excuse a violation of the law of tithe based on the failure of the priesthood. That explains why Malachi was able on the one hand to condemn the sin of the priests, and on the other hand still to require the people to bring their tithes to the temple.

Malachi reinforces what the rest of the Old Testament teaches about the nature and purpose of tithing. Tithe belongs to the Lord. He used it to provide for the priests and Levites, and no one had the right to keep it to himself or herself. Robbing God was a sin committed against the Lord, not against the temple or the priesthood. Therefore, tithe is required by the Lord in spite of the spiritual deterioration of those who benefit by it. In His own time He will call them to account.

Tithing in the New Testament

The New Testament has very little to say about tithing, but what it says is significant for the Christian. There is no explicit command to tithe in the New Testament, but neither is there a rejection of the system.

The longest discussion of tithing in the New Testament is recorded in Hebrews 7:1-10. The author is analyzing the encounter between Abraham and Melchizedek, and making certain significant theological points in his argument. The fact that Abraham returned his tithe to Melchizedek is taken as clear evidence of the superiority of the priesthood of Melchizedek over the Aaronic one. The passage presupposes that tithing is a divinely ordained practice. There is no rejection of tithing; rather an implicit recognition of its value and significance.

The other references to the tithe are found in the Gospels.

Jesus mentions it in Luke 18:12 in the context of the parable about the Pharisee and the tax collector. They both went to the temple to pray: the Pharisee with a spirit of self-righteousness, the tax collector with humility seeking God's mercy. The Pharisee mentioned giving a tenth of everything he received as evidence of his great piety.

Jesus condemned the self-righteousness of the Pharisee. When religious acts are used for self-glorification, they lose their value and become empty formalities. Tithing was used by the Pharisee as a means of earning God's mercy. According to Jesus, that is not the purpose of tithing. God's mercy is a free gift received in faith and humility. The one who thought he had paid for God's mercy, went out empty handed. The tax collector, who considered himself a great sinner in need of God's grace, received mercy. The Pharisee misused tithe in his religious experience.

Tithe is mentioned also in Matthew 22:23 and in its parallel in Luke 11:42. Jesus condemned the Pharisees for being extremely careful in tithing, yet neglecting "justice and the love of God" (11:42). Or, as Matthew puts it, "neglecting the more important matters of the law—justice, mercy, and faithfulness" (22:23). Jesus is echoing Amos's message: religious zeal and a commitment to justice, mercy, and love must be kept together. Then he added: "You should have practiced the latter without neglecting the other [tithing]." Here was a clear endorsement of tithing on the part of Jesus.[33] In approving tithing, though, "he judges it insufficient of itself."[34]

Jesus never rejected tithing itself, but condemned its misuse. He defined it in terms of what it really is: a response to God's transforming grace.

Paul did not mention tithing in his epistles. However, he addressed the issue of providing for those who preach the gospel: "Don't you know that those who work in the temple get their food from the temple and those who serve the altar share in what is offered on the altar? In the same way, the Lord has commanded that those who preach the gospel should receive their living from the gospel" (1 Corinthians 9:13).

Paul was referring primarily to the Old Testament tithing system. He drew a parallel between priests and Levites and those who were proclaiming the gospel. The point he argued is that the gospel workers should be provided with their living in the same way as was done in the priestly system. What was particularly important was that this was described by Paul as a direct command to the church from the Lord Himself. The apostle told the church that in reference to the tithe (according to the Lord), "we ought not do less than the Jewish law requires."[35] Thus, he implicitly endorsed Christian tithing.

For the Christian, tithing is not just an Old Testament practice with no relevance for believers, but part of the Christian understanding of true stewardship. In fact, "the practice of Christian tithing grows out of the Hebrew tradition, and it is there that we discover its rich meanings."[36]

On the matter of tithing, the New Testament shows a conformity with the Old Testament principle of returning to God a tenth of everything we earn, and reminds us of its purpose and significance. The New Testament condemns tithing as a manifestation of self-righteousness and challenges the believer to also practice justice, mercy, and love. The basic purpose of tithing remains the same: the Lord uses it to provide for those who dedicate their lives to the proclamation of the gospel. The theological significance of tithing in the Old Testament lies at the very foundation of Christian tithing.

Summary and Conclusions

The Old Testament provides a *theological foundation* for tithing that makes this practice an enriching one in the life of the believer. The first element in this foundation is the perception and understanding of God as Creator of heaven and earth. In the context of tithing, the purpose of this statement is not to emphasize God's majestic power but His ownership of all the universe. The cosmos belongs to one Person, the One who brought it into existence. Any creature who claims ownership in any way is usurping God's right.

The second aspect of the person and work of God that provides a theological basis for tithing is His providential care, guidance, and love toward us. The Creator has not abandoned His creatures to the forces of evil. In a hostile world of sin and death, He still remains the Owner who opposes evil in order to preserve our lives. This providential care presupposes God's work of redemption through which we are restored to full fellowship with Him in Christ. Evil was defeated through Christ, and now we can participate in His victory. Life was preserved for us through the Son, and it is also through Him that we receive God's blessings and find all of our needs supplied. Everything belongs to

God, not only by creation, but also by redemption. His providential power continues to preserve the universe. There is no aspect of human life, no need we may have, that He cannot supply for us.

The *nature of tithe* can be properly stated in one phrase: it is holy. Holiness points to that which is unique, different, and therefore belongs to the Holy One. There is no one like Him in the universe because He is the Creator. Since tithe is holy, we cannot retain it but must return it to God. From a human point of view, tithe appears to be part of our income, even something earned through our work and effort. But here the theological foundation becomes relevant for us by reminding us that everything we have comes from the Lord. We are responsible to administer all the gifts He has given us, except the tenth, which is exclusively His and must be returned to Him. Tithe has been endowed with holiness by God.

Tithing has several important purposes. First, through the tithe God allows His people (not just the priests) to deal with the holy, to handle that which belongs to Him. In a sense, this is a democratization of a priestly function. When dealing with the holy, we are challenged to be holy. God's call to believers is partially based on an ethic of imitation. He said to His people, "You are to be holy to me because I, the Lord, am holy" (Leviticus 20:26). Tithing makes a contribution toward that glorious goal, because in our giving we are imitating God. In the process, self is subdued and the love of God fills the human heart.

Second, since tithe is holy, it becomes a test of loyalty for every person. It is a test because it sets limits to our freedom by calling our attention to our dependence on God. Not everything to which we have access is ours. As we indicated before, tithe is a test because it appears to be part of our income, and, therefore, we can be tempted to keep it for ourselves, thereby violating its holiness. In a sense, tithe is analogous to the tree of the knowledge of good and evil in the Garden of Eden. Adam and Eve had free access to eat from all the trees in the garden except one. That tree became a test of their loyalty to God.

Third, tithing reminds us of our covenant with the Lord, of our total, unconditional surrender to His loving will. In the covenant relationship, God becomes our God and we become His people; He is recognized as our Savior, the One who would bless us. In our relationship, we humbly recognize that all we have belongs to Him and that our spiritual and economic needs will be supplied by Him. Tithe is a symbol, or a reminder, of that total commitment to the Lord. When we stretch out our hand and reverently deposit our tithe in the offering plate during the worship service, we are giving the Lord a fraction of our life as a token of our total consecration to Him.

We can easily conclude that tithing is a witness to the trusting and loving relationship established with our Lord and Savior. That is probably why individuals in the Bible stopped tithing when their relationship with the Lord was broken through apostasy.

Finally, tithing has an additional purpose assigned to it by God (and not by man). Through it, God provided for the needs of those He called to be His ministers. God is the only one who determines the way tithe is to be used. This has serious implications for those who faithfully return tithes to the Lord. We should never conclude that tithe is a payment made for services received from a minister. That would immediately open the door for its commercialization. Under such circumstances, the individual may feel free to use the tithe "to pay" only those whose services were what was wanted or expected. If so, we would be using tithe to control the quality of the product we wanted. This would contradict the very heart, nature, and purpose of tithing. Tithe always is to be returned to the Lord because it is holy, and it is He who invests it or determines how it is to be used—never us.

Therefore, it is never justifiable to stop tithing based on the real or apparent failure of God's ministers. When God's people assumed that attitude, He rebuked them strongly, accusing them of robbing Him. Even withholding tithe in order to motivate a reform in the church becomes a violation of God's purpose for tithe. It is not our prerogative to determine by ourselves how and for what purpose to use the tithe.

Having said that, we must point out that God's ministers have a solemn responsibility as the recipients of tithes. The Lord expects them to fulfill their responsibilities in an efficient way that provides for the needs of the church and the proclamation of the gospel. God's plan for His church is to have both church members and ministers fulfill their respective duties properly. Everything must be done to try, as much as possible, to have all "Judah" pleased with the ministry of their spiritual leaders.

STEWARDSHIP AND THE THEOLOGY OF TITHE

Follow-through Discussion for Tithing in the Old Testament

1. What analogy can one derive from the fact that Melchizedek's blessing preceded Abraham's tithing? (See Genesis 14.)

2. What did Jacob's vow express to the Lord? (See Genesis 28:10-22.)

3. What is the purpose of the tithing legislation as expressed in Leviticus 27:30-33?

4. In Numbers 18:21-32, what is the significance of the verb *rûm* (translated "present") and the word *terumah* (translated "an offering")?

5. Discuss the significant differences between the tithe legislation found in Deuteronomy, and the tithe legislation found in Leviticus and Numbers. What conclusion can be drawn from these differences?

6. Discuss the significance of tithing being a part of the covenant renewal in the time of Nehemiah. (See Nehemiah 10:38,39; 12:44; 13:5,12.)

7. In Malachi, what important religious statements were the people making in not bringing their tithes to the Lord?

Follow-Through Discussion for Tithing in the New Testament

1. From the longest discussion about tithing in the New Testament (Hebrews 7:1-10), what conclusion can be made regarding the priesthood of Melchizedek?
2. Discuss the theological foundations for tithing as provided in the

Old and New Testaments.

3. What important spiritual purposes can be found in the tithing system?

[The following additional materials on tithing and related topics have been produced by GC Church Ministries during 1991-1994: *Life Principles, SDA Financial Systems, Tithing Moments, Stewardship and Strategic Planning.*]

ENDNOTES

1. For an evaluation of those studies see Menahem Herman, *Tithe as a Gift: The Institution in the Pentateuch and in Light of Mauso's Presentation Theory* (San Francisco, CA: Mellen Research University Press, 1991), pp 7-37.
2. See Jacob Milgrom, *Numbers: The JPS Torah Commentary* (New York: Jewish Publication Society, 1990), p 432. See also Gary A. Anderson's *Sacrifices and Offerings in Ancient Israel* (Atlanta, GA: Scholars Press, 1987), pp 78-80. We should mention that a nonreligious royal tithe (tax) was known in Israel (see 1 Sam 8:10-17; Anderson, ibid, pp 81, 82).
3. Jacob Milgrom, *Cult and Conscience* (Leiden: E J Brill, 1976), p 58. Milgrom's discussion is based on a study prepared by M A Dandamayev, "Chramowaja Desjatina W Pozdnej Babilonii," Vestnik Drevney Istorii (1965), 14-34. See also M A Dandamayev, "State and Temple in Babylonia in the First Millennium B C," in *State and Temple Economy in the Ancient Near East*, E Lipinsky, ed (Leuven: Department Orientalistick, 1979), pp 593, 594.
4. Consult J A MacCulloh, "Tithes," *Encyclopaedia of Religion and Ethics*, edited by James Hasting, vol 12 (Edinburgh: T & T Clark, m.d.), p 347; W H D Rouse, "Tithes (Greek)," ibid, pp 350, 351; and G Hawthorne, "*Tithe*," *New International Dictionary of New Testament Theology*, edited by Colin Brown, vol 3 (Grand Rapids, MI: Zondervan Publisher, 1978), p 851.
5. E G White, *The SDA Bible Commentary*, vol 1, p 1093 (*Testimonies*, vol 3, p 393).
6. E G White, *Testimonies to the Church*, vol 3, p 388.
7. E E Carpenter, "Tithe," *International Standard Bible Encyclopedia*, vol 4 (Grand Rapids, MI: W B Eerdmans, 1988), p 862.
8. E G White, *Patriarchs and Prophets*, p 187.
9. Walter Brueggemann, *Genesis* (Atlanta: John Knox, 1982), p 248.
10. On the general structure of the chapter consult, G J Wenham, *The Book of Leviticus* (Grand Rapids, MI: W B Eerdmans, 1979), pp 336, 337.
11. Baruch A Levine, *Leviticus: The JPS Torah Commentary* (New York: Jewish Publication Society, 1989), p 192.
12. B Beck, "Baqar," *Theological Dictionary of the Old Testament*, vol 2 (Grand Rapids, MI: W B Eerdmans, 1975), p 210.
13. This aspect of tithing is emphasized by Herman, *Tithe*, p 60. He goes too far when he argues that "the tithe ordinances of Leviticus describe a systematic reciprocity under the covenant through which tangible goods are exchanged for divine protection" (ibid). He is commercializing tithe. The basic reason given in Leviticus for tithing is that tithe is holy. Of course, it presupposes God's blessings, but it does not determine or force God to bless the people.
14. *The SDA Bible Commentary*, vol 1, p 818.
15. Philip J Budd, *Numbers* (Waco, TX: Word Books, 1984), p 201.
16. See Milgrom, *Numbers*, pp 148-154.
17. This interpretation was suggested by J Milgrom, "Heave Offering," *Interpreter's Dictionary of the Bible Supplementary Volume* (Nashville, TN: Abingdon, 1976), p 391.
18. Milgrom, among others, has argued for the mandatory nature of tithe in Numbers

18 (*Numbers*, p 433).
19. Peter C Craigie, *Deuteronomy* (Grand Rapids, MI: W B Eerdmans, 1976), p 229.
20. The prevailing interpretation among scholars who deny the Mosaic authorship of the Pentateuch is that we are dealing here in Deuteronomy with a source written after the exile, reflecting the nature and purpose of tithing during that period. They argue that the legislation recorded in Leviticus regulates the use of tithe during the exile or shortly before the exile. See Herman, *Tithe,* pp 7-37.
21. E G White, *Patriarchs and Prophets*, p 530.
22. The third day mentioned in this verse may refer to the third day after the people arrived at the cultic center; but this is far from certain. It may well be that tithing practices in the northern kingdom were somewhat different from those in Judah. See Hans Walter Wolff, *Joel and Amos* (Philadelphia: Fortress Press, 1977), p 219.
23. Shalom M Paul, *Amos*, (Minneapolis: Fortress Press, 1991), p 139.
24. Wolff, *Joel and Amos*, p 219.
25. We do not know the procedure followed in the distribution of tithe to the Levites. Nehemiah 10:37, 38 gives the impression that during the post-exilic period the only tithe brought to the temple was the Levitical tithe of the tithe for the priests, and that the tithe itself was storaged in the towns where the Levites could obtain what they needed. However, those two verses are not as clear as we would want them to be, because they seem to be in some tension with a couple of other passages in Nehemiah. In 12:44 "the portions required by the law for the priests and the Levites" were brought to the storerooms of the temple by selected individuals. These "portions" would have included the tithe, as suggested by 12:47. (The Israelites "set aside the portion for the other Levites [in addition to the singers and gatekeepers], and the Levites set aside the portion for the descendants of Aaron.") Nehemiah 13:5 states that "the tithes of grain, new wine and oil provided for the Levites, singers and gatekeepers, as well as the contribution for the priests" and were kept in the storerooms of the temple. See also Malachi 3:10. It is quite possible that Nehemiah 10:38 is simply stating that the Levites were being instructed to bring their own tithes (the tithe of the tithe) to the temple but that the people were allowed to bring their tithe to a central place in their own towns. The other passages would then indicate that, in fact, all tithe went to the temple, for storage. Having said that, one could guess also that some of the Levitical tithe, for instance the tithe of herds and flocks and perhaps of some of the produce of the earth, were stored in central places throughout the land (e.g., the Levitical cities) and used by the Levites as needed. It may not be wrong to conclude that the only tithe stored in the temple was the tithe of grain, new wine, and oil.
26. See H G M Williamson, *Ezra, Nehemiah* (Waco: TX: Word Books, 1985), p 387.
27. E G White, *Prophets and Kings*, p 670.
28. Ibid.
29. D J Clines, *Ezra, Nehemiah, Esther* (Grand Rapids, MI: W B Eerdmans, 1984), p 120.
30. William L Holladay, *A Concise Hebrew and Aramaic Lexicon of the Old Testament* (Grand Rapids, MI: W B Eerdmans, 1971), p 338.
31. Raymond A Bowman wrote, "It was apparently presumed that it was the Levite's obligation to serve, just as it was the layman's to contribute" ("The Book of

Nehemiah," *Interpreter's Bible*, vol 3 [Nashville, TN: Abingdon Press, 1954]), p 810.
32. See, among others, *The SDA Bible Commentary*, vol 4, p 1121; Ralph L Smith, Micah-Malachi (Waco, TX: Word Books, 1984), p 298; Elizabeth Achtemeier, Nahum-Malachi (Atlanta: John Knox Press, 1986), p 171; Pieter A Verhoef, *The Books of Haggai and Malachi* (Grand Rapids, MI: W B Eerdmans, 1987), p 158.
33. Leiland Wilson, "The Old Testament and Tithe," *Baker's Dictionary of Practical Theology* (Grand Rapids, MI: Baker Book House, 1967), p 357.
34. Achtemeier, *Malachi*, p 192.
35. Wilson, *"Tithe,"* p 357. For more on 1 Corinthians 9:13, see next chapter.
36. Ibid.

STEWARDSHIP AND THE THEOLOGY OF OFFERINGS

Introduction

The study of ancient religions suggests that in the interaction between humans and the divine, bringing an offering to the gods was a constitutive aspect of personal devotion. Throughout the ancient Near East different types of offerings were brought to the gods by humans who sought their blessings, protection, forgiveness, and guidance. In most cases the offerings were visualized as means of supplying the needs of the gods in order to win or preserve their favor.[1] This intense concern for presenting material offerings to the gods was universal.

Biblical religion is not an exception in this area of worship praxis. Indeed, offerings play a significant role in the sanctuary services of the Old Testament and in the Christian worship of the New Testament. We will explore in this article the richness of the biblical materials on this subject. In some cases we will pay attention to the terminology used to refer to offerings, but our main interest will focus on the different types of offerings mentioned in the Bible. We will explore primarily the main theological or religious ideas associated with those offerings in order to summarize the fundamental elements of the theology and practice of offerings in the Bible.

Offerings in the Old Testament

The Old Testament mentions offerings much more often than tithe. In a book interested in the worship of the only and true God, offerings have a very distinctive place and function. Worship and offerings are practically inseparable in the Old Testament.

In what follows we will discuss the different types of offerings mentioned in the Old Testament.

Sacrificial Expiatory Offerings

Expiation and sacrificial offerings are linked together in the Old Testament system of worship. The primary expiatory offerings were the sin-offering (Leviticus 4) and the guilt offering (Leviticus 5), called "offerings" in Numbers 5:9 and 18:8. The Hebrew term used there is *terûmāh*, a noun possibly derived from the verbal root *rûm* = "be high," which in one of its verbal forms means "donate, set aside." It designates a gift or an offering set aside for the Lord outside the sanctuary, then brought to the sanctuary and given to God.[2]

The expiatory power of these offerings was not located in the sacrificial victim itself, but in God, who, out of His grace, assigned that function to them (Leviticus 17:11). In other words, the atoning efficacy was located in God's willingness to forgive the sins of His people (see Leviticus 4:26, 31).

The sacrificial expiatory offerings seemed to have had a limited function. In fact, their only function was to point to God as the only One who could expiate sin. The Old Testament itself testifies to the ultimate inefficacy of the expiatory offerings to bring forgiveness, and at the same time identifies the only effective means of atonement. David recognized that his sin could not be removed through sacrificial offerings of animals (Psalm 51:16). His only hope was to rely exclusively on God's "unfailing love" and compassion (verses 1, 2). When it comes to the redemption of human life, no sacrificial animal is costly enough to accomplish it: "No man can redeem the life of another or give to God a ransom for him—the ransom for a life is costly, no payment is ever enough—that he should live on forever and not see decay" (Psalm 49:7-9).[3]

It is impossible for humans to bring an offering to the Lord costly enough to ransom themselves. God is the only One who could provide that offering, and He did. Isaiah foresaw the future work of the Messiah, who, although rejected by His people, was God's expiatory offering provided by Him for their redemption. The Lord made "his life a guilt offering" (Isaiah 53:10); He bore the sin of many and was numbered with the transgressors (verse 12) in order to declare them righteous (verse 11).

What no human offering could accomplish the divine offering achieved. This is further developed in the New Testament, where we are informed that it is impossible for the blood of sacrificial victims to remove sin from the worshipers (Hebrews 10:4). This is possible solely through the blood of Christ (10:14). Paul states that God "presented him as a sacrifice of atonement, through faith in his blood" (Romans 3:25). Christ himself interpreted His mission as giving "his life as a ransom for many" (Mark 10:45).

The importance of this understanding of expiatory offerings is foundational for a biblical theology of offerings. First, God is described here as willing to give, as an "offerer." This provides a theological platform for human giving. Human giving is to model itself after divine giving. Compared to how much God gives, His people give Him very little.[4] But what is important for us to understand is that if we are expected to bring an offering to Him, it is because He Himself gave an offering on our behalf.

Second, none of our offerings has an expiatory function. We possess nothing we could bring to the Lord to make us acceptable before Him, and we do not need to do so, because God provided the only offering through which expiation is achieved. Our offerings should never be viewed as attempts on our part to obtain God's sympathy, love, or forgiveness. That is the exclusive and indisputable function of God's offering of Christ for us. The motivation of our giving should never be to make ourselves meritorious before the Lord. In fact, what makes our offerings acceptable to God is the sacrificial offering of His Son, who sanctifies our giving.

Sacrifices as Offerings

Apart from the sin and guilt offerings, there are other sacrificial offerings that, in addition to the expiatory function, also had other theological and religious purposes. Two of them are of particular value to our study; namely, the burnt (Leviticus 1) and the peace (Leviticus 3) offerings. We will deal only with the nonexpiatory aspect of these offerings.

Burnt Offerings (Leviticus 1:3-17)

No part of this offering was given to the priest or to the one bringing the offering; the whole sacrificial victim was burnt on the altar, totally surrendered to the Lord (Leviticus 1:9). Scholars have detected in this sacrifice a ritual expression of the willingness of the worshippers to commit or reconsecrate their whole lives to God. He, as their Lord, had a total claim on them, and this offering was a symbolic act of complete self-surrender to Him.[5]

The burnt offering is referred to in Hebrew as a *qorbān* = "offering," from the verb *qārab* = "come near, approach." This is a generic term used to designate sacrifices and other offerings brought by the Israelites to the Lord (see Leviticus 22:18; Numbers 7:3, 12 17; 15:4; 31:50). It could be translated as "that which is brought near, presented, offered."[6] An offering is, therefore, something that is transferred from our sphere to the Lord's; by bringing it near to Him, it becomes His.

Of particular interest to us is the fact that different animals are accepted as sacrificial victims for a burnt offering. The animals are listed on the basis of their financial value. The most valuable is mentioned first, a young bull, and is followed by sheep and goats (see Leviticus 1:3, 10). Even birds, a dove, or a pigeon could be offered (verse 14).

Two comments are in order here. First, an offering is something that is costly to the worshipers. They are depriving themselves of a costly and useful animal by giving it to the Lord.[7] David understood this principle and rejected the idea of giving to the Lord a sacrificial victim that was not his (2 Samuel 24:24). Second, God does not expect everyone to give the same amount. Naming the sacrificial victims from the most to the least expensive makes it possible for everyone to bring something to the Lord. The Lord would expect some to bring a bull and others a sheep or a goat, depending on their financial condition. The poorest of all could bring a bird (see Leviticus 5:7; 12:8).[8] The theological implication is that God considers the inner disposition of the giver, and that the willingness to worship Him has more value than the monetary worth of the offering.[9] One's internal experience would be expressed in bringing to the Lord the best one can offer.

Besides the expiatory function of this sacrifice, two other reasons are given for bringing it to the Lord. Leviticus 22:17-20 describes a votive offering and a freewill offering. A votive offering was brought after the fulfillment of a vow. A person presented a request to the Lord and solemnly promised to give a votive offering after receiving an answer to the prayer.[10] Bringing this offering was a joyful occasion, during which the person expressed gratitude to the Lord who answers prayers (see Psalm 61:8; Nahum 1:15).[11] The burnt offering could also be a voluntary offering. It was, then, brought to the Lord "out of devotion, not because of precept or promise";[12] an expression of love to God.

Based on our previous comments, we can conclude that an offering is a tangible expression of a person's full commitment to the Lord brought to Him out of gratitude and love. It is to be brought to the center of worship and handed over to those appointed by God to receive it. One is expected to bring the very best one can offer based on one's financial resources.

Peace Offerings (Leviticus 3:1-17)

The peace offering was distinguished from the burnt offering in several ways. The sacrificial victim could be a female from the herd or the flock. Female animals were more expensive. Most of the flesh of the sacrificial victim was given back to the worshiper to eat in the company of the family and friends (Leviticus 7:11-21). When bringing the burnt offering, the individual did not benefit materially; but in the case of the peace offering, he or she did benefit. This allowed for a group to come together to worship God.

There were three types of peace offerings: the votive, the freewill, and the thanksgiving offerings (Leviticus 7:12, 16). All of them were voluntary offerings. They could be brought to fulfill a vow or as an act of personal devotion to God, similar to the burnt offering. The new element is the thanksgiving aspect. The Hebrew *tôdāh* = "thanksgiving" is used in the Bible to express the ideas of praise, thanksgiving, and confession.[13] The offering was presented after experiencing deliverance from some danger. It was "a product of the spontaneous desire to perform a public deed expressing one's thankfulness for blessings that have been enjoyed."[14] The occasion was to be joyful (Deuteronomy 27:7: Psalm 95:2).[15]

A couple of new elements are introduced here to clarify the meaning of offerings in the Old Testament. First, this offering can be of material benefit to those who offer it. As we noticed, most of it is given back to the giver to facilitate collective worship with family members and friends. All share, or participate, in the offering brought by one of them. Second, the offering could be a vehicle to express thanksgiving and praise to God for His blessings and power to deliver from evil. It was in essence an expression of gratitude to the covenant God.

Other Offerings

Several other offerings are mentioned in the Old Testament. The "meal offering" is called in Hebrew *minchāh* and means "a gift, tribute." In Leviticus this is a technical term used to designate a cereal offering made of fine flour, cooked or uncooked, and mixed with oil (Leviticus 2:1-10). It was given to the Lord, but He gave most of it to the officiating priest.

In the Old Testament, the term *minchāh* designates a gift given to a superior who was recognized as master or ruler over the person bringing the gift (see Judges 3:15; 2 Samuel 8:2, 6). By bringing a *minchāh* = "meal offering" to God, the Israelites were stating in ritual language that Yahweh was their covenant Lord and they were His subjects.[16] The fact that it was a grain offering may suggest that the fruits of the land were recognized to be the result of the blessings of the Lord.[17] Notice, however, that what was brought was not the grain but flour. Through their work they transformed the grain into flour. God and humans are working together, and when humans bring an offering, they are not only recognizing the work of God but also consecrating their own work to Him.[18]

The Israelites were required to bring to the Lord the first fruits of the land (Leviticus 23:9-11; Numbers 18:12, 13; Deuteronomy 18:4; 26:1-11). This offering was essentially a thanksgiving offering given to the Lord for the support of the priesthood (Deuteronomy 18:3-5).[19] The fact that it was called the first fruits suggests that it was the very best of the harvest (Numbers 18:12; Exodus 23:19). It also indicates that God was first in the life of the worshiper. The Israelites did not give from the surplus.[20] Before they began to enjoy the harvest, they separated the first fruits for the Lord (Leviticus 23:14).[21]

This offering was a recognition of the fact that the fertility of the land was in the hands of the Lord, and that He was "the source of the bounty"[22] and the owner of the land (Deuteronomy 26:10).[23] The theological emphasis of this offering was on the goodness of the Lord, who promised the land and its fruits to the people, and fulfilled His promises (Deuteronomy 26:3, 8-10).[24] The Israelites joyfully celebrated God's faithfulness manifested in the gift of the land and in the blessing of the harvest (Leviticus 23:11).[25] In this context a reference to the redemption from Egypt is of particular importance, because it preceded God's giving the land to the people and was the foundation upon which was based the offerings and gifts the people brought to God (Deuteronomy 26:8-10).

Bringing this offering to the temple was an extremely joyful occasion (Deuteronomy 26:11). This was a collective experience of joy in which the people, the Levites, and the aliens dwelling among them were involved in celebrating the fact that God gave them all those goods. This offering was an outward expression of a profound faith in the Lord and of deep religious feelings of gratitude.[26]

An offering was also required from the spoils of war (Numbers 31:29, 41, 52). Several different terms are used to designate this offering. It is called a *mekes* = "Cultic dues or levy" (verses 28, 37, 41), a *terûmāh* = "a gift" (verses 29, 52), and a *qorbān* = "what is brought near" (verse 50). By sharing the spoils of war with the priests and Levites, the Israelites were recognizing that it was God who gave them victory over their enemies. Therefore, the offering was an expression of gratitude for victory.[27]

The three offerings discussed in this section reinforce what we have found already and add some new elements to the content and meaning of offerings in the Bible. Worship, joy, gratitude, and thanksgiving characterize all the offerings, even though some of them are required offerings. God is recognized as the One who blesses and protects His people, their work, and the land. Through these offerings God is praised as the Lord of Israel, to whom one should bring the first and the best of the harvest. He is proclaimed to be the Owner of the land who fulfilled the promises made to His people by blessing them with the land and the harvest.

Special Offerings

A special offering is one brought to the Lord for a specific purpose. The best example of this type of offering in the Old Testament is the one collected for the building of the tabernacle. The Lord requested it from each individual (Exodus 25:2); yet, it was to be a freewill offering (36:3). Giving was to be the expression of an inward attitude in which the center of the personality of the individual was to be involved. Only those whose "hearts prompted" (*nādab* = "urge, give voluntarily") them to give were to bring this offering (Exodus 25:2; 35:5). The internal disposition is also expressed by the phrase "whose heart was lifted" (Exodus 35:21) or "whose spirit was prompted" (verse 29). The request of the Lord was to find in the hearts of the people a positive response, and it did. Consequently, they brought as an offering gold, silver, bronze, precious stones, yarn, fine linen, skins of animals, wood, olive oil, and spices (Exodus 25:2-7). Everyone, men and women, brought something from their possessions (Exodus 35:5); in fact, they brought more than was needed (Exodus 36:6, 7).

This special offering is called a *terûmāh*, a gift dedicated to God and then brought to the Lord. All the offerings were taken to a central place and given to Moses, who was responsible for distributing and administering them for the intended project.

When the first group of exiles was ready to return to Jerusalem in 539 BC, their neighbors provided for them gifts, freewill offerings, to be used in rebuilding the temple (Ezra 1:6). In 457 BC, Ezra returned with another group of exiles. This time the king, his advisors and officers, and the Jews gave a donation (*terûmāh* = "gift") to support the temple services (8:25). Ezra kept careful records of this offering (8:26-30).

Whenever the temple needed repairs, an offering was collected from the people for that purpose. In 2 Chronicles 24:6, 9, such an offering is called a *maś'ēth*. This noun is based on the verb *nāsā,'* which means "to lift, carry," suggesting that the noun designates a gift or an offering as "something that is carried to someone else," in this case to the Lord.[28] During the time of King Joash, when the temple was being repaired, a chest was placed outside the temple to collect this offering. The Bible states that the people brought this freewill offerings joyfully (2 Chronicles 24:10).[29]

A special offering was requested by the Lord during the dedication of the altar and the sanctuary (Numbers 7). Each tribe sent their gifts (*qorbān*, verse 3) through their representatives. Their gifts consisted of sacrificial animals, utensils of gold and silver, flour, and incense, which were needed to begin the sanctuary services.[30] The Israelites were responsible for providing enough resources to operate the sanctuary services, and they fulfilled that responsibility through their offerings.

Three times a year the Israelites made a pilgrimage to Jerusalem to celebrate the feasts of Unleavened Bread, Weeks, and Tabernacles (Deuteronomy 16:16). On each of those occasions they were expected to bring to the Lord an offering called *mattānāh* = "a gift," from the verb *nāthan* = "to give," which designates, among other things, a gift given by a father to his child (see Genesis 25:6) and God's gift of the priesthood to Aaron (Numbers 18:7; compare verses 6 and 29). It was very often a gift prompted by a good and loving disposition of one person toward another (compare Esther 9:22).

In the context of these three offerings, Deuteronomy 16:16, 17, makes several important statements. The first: "No man [person] should appear before the Lord empty-handed" (verse 16). Offerings have a place in collective worship. When coming before God the people were to bring something to Him as a testimony to the reception of His blessings. These were to be freewill offerings (verse 10), expressing one's joy for God's care and protection. The second principle: "Each of you must bring a gift in proportion to the way the Lord your God has blessed you" (verse 17). A literal translation of the last part of that sentence would be, "like the blessing of the Lord your God, which He gave to you." The amount of the offering would differ from person to person, because it would be based on the principle of proportionality—the amount reflected (was in proportion to) how much the Lord had blessed the individual. The third element: ". . . which He gave to you" (see verse 17), indicates that divine giving precedes and makes possible human giving. The text implies that God gives His blessings to everyone, and that when a person comes before Him, he or she would always have a *reason* and *something* to give to the Lord (compare Ezekiel 46:5, 11).

It is interesting to notice that the special offerings we have just discussed, as well as the other offerings, were required or requested by God, and yet they were to be freewill expressions of joy and gratitude. It seems as if God was using the system of offerings to teach the Israelites how to express joy, gratitude, and many other feelings of devotion to Him. Surprisingly, the Lord interpreted the neglect to bring offerings to Him as an act of robbery (Malachi 3:6-8). This was probably based on the principle that if God blessed the people, He had the right to a gift of gratitude from them through which He was recognized as their Lord. In this way He protected them from falling into the heinous sin of idolatry. To deprive Him of offerings would be tantamount to a rejection of His Lordship over them, crediting the blessings received from Him to some other power. Those for whom Yahweh was the only God would simply bring offerings to Him. An offering presupposes a strong personal commitment. It should not surprise us to find a connection between a spiritual reform and an increase in offerings (2 Chronicles 31:1, 10-14).

The Old Testament points to a time when kings and foreign powers will bring gifts or offerings to the Lord (see Psalm 68:29; 76:11; Isaiah 18:7). The Hebrew term for this offering is *shay* = "gift, present," and designates an offering given by the powerful and rich to the One who is identified as the universal Lord victorious in war.[31]

The special offerings we have discussed seem to emphasize in a special way the importance of the inner disposition of the individual that moves him or her to give a freewill offering. This disposition, accompanied by feelings of joy, gratitude, thanksgiving, and worship, embodies itself in the concrete act of bringing an offering to the Lord. In this act He is recognized and proclaimed as Lord over the lives of those who worship Him and as the Owner of the land and of its produce. David summarized this concept well when he wrote: "But who am I, and who are my people, that we should be able to give as generously as this? Everything comes from you, and we have given you only what comes from your hand" (1 Chronicles 29:14).[32]

Offerings in the New Testament

There are very few references to offerings in the New Testament, although the verb "to give" (*didōmi*) is used extensively. What is particularly impressive is that about 25 percent of the time the verb *didōmi* is used, and it has God as its subject.[33] God is the One who gives us our daily bread (Luke 11:3), rain, crops, food (Acts 14:17), life, and everything we need (Acts 17:25). He gives us repentance (Acts 11:18), victory (1 Corinthians 15:57), grace (1 Peter 5:5), love (1 John 3:1), wisdom (James 1:5), the Holy Spirit (John 3:34; Acts 5:32), spiritual gifts (1 Corinthians 12:7-10), an inheritance (Acts 20:32), the kingdom (Luke 12:32), and eternal life (1 John 5:4). In a very special and unique way God gave His Son (John 3:16), the Bread of Life (6:32), who gave His life to ransom ours (Matthew 20:28; 1 Timothy 2:6), by giving "himself for our sins" (Galatians 1:4).

God and Christ are described in the New Testament as the Great Givers who enrich humans out of their loving grace. Hence, Christ was able to challenge His followers to give freely because they received freely (Matthew 10:8). The purpose of Christian giving is not to supply God's needs, because God does not need anything (Acts 17:25). Our giving makes us more like our Lord.

Jesus and Offerings

Jesus instructed His followers concerning the nature and spirit of true giving. The gospel provides for us several incidents in His life where He addressed this important subject. We have grouped them here under different subheadings.

Offerings and Worship

When Christ was born, an offering was brought to him by an unexpected group of persons. Some non-Jews came from the East to meet Him and gave Him gifts of gold, incense, and myrrh (Matthew 2:1-11). These "wise men" belonged to an Eastern class of well-educated, wealthy, and influential people called *mágoi* = "magi." In general, they were known to be experts in astrology and the interpretation of dreams.[34] Matthew understood them to be learned men who were able to identify the signs of the birth of Jesus, and having done so, went out to seek Him.[35] They had come into contact with the Hebrew Scriptures and believed in the Messianic prophecies found there (see Numbers 24:17).

The magi did not come to Jesus empty-handed; but rather, brought with them gifts for the new king. The term *dōron* = "gift, offering" is the Greek equivalent for the Hebrew term *qorb_n*, used in the Old Testament to refer to gifts and sacrificial offerings (see Hebrews 5:1). In this particular case, these were gifts of homage. They had come, according to their own words, "to worship him" (Matthew 2:2). The act of worship could be understood as "signifying homage and submission" to the Messianic king.[36] But in the context of Matthew, "Jesus is the manifestation of God's presence (Matthew 1:23), the Son of God (2:15) in a unique sense, and thus One to be worshiped."[37]

In this passage, the costly gift/offering is associated with the concepts of worship, homage, and submission. Such gifts are tangible expressions of those feelings and attitudes. Through their offerings the magi were recognizing the greatness and superiority of this great King of Israel.

Offerings and Interpersonal Relationships

Jesus, like the prophets of the Old Testament, did not separate religious devotion, expressed by bringing an offering to the Lord, from proper ethical and social interaction. An offering reflected not only a state of peace with God but also with one's covenant community. Living in harmony with others was almost a prerequisite for an offering. This seems to be what Jesus meant when he said: "If you are offering your gift at the altar and there remember that your brother has something against you, leave your gift there in front of the altar. First go and be reconciled to your brother; then come and offer your gift" (Matthew 5:23, 24). An offering loses its value as an expression of love and gratitude to God if it comes from a heart at war with others. The vertical and horizontal dimensions of our religious experience intersect in the act of worship through an offering.

Another aspect of the link between offerings and how we relate to others is contained in Jesus' criticism of the Jewish practice of the Corban (Mark 7:10-12). A person could devote to the Lord his or her possessions making them unavailable to any other member of the family. By arguing that it would be a violation of the vow to use the property or possession to alleviate their needs,[38] one could build a case for neglecting one's parents. Jesus condemned this practice, arguing that it violated the fifth commandment. The principle exemplified here seems to be that being a good steward also means providing for the needs of our relatives. In other words, our giving to God should be balanced by our responsibility to our families, because caring for them and supplying their needs is part of our religious experience.

Offerings and Commitment to the Lord

Giving an offering to God is not automatically a reflection of our absolute commitment to Him. The poor widow brought a freewill offering to the temple possibly as an expression of gratitude and love to God (Luke 21:1-4). The rich also brought their freewill offerings. Jesus compared and evaluated their giving and selected the offering of the widow as a true gift. His eyes perceived that the wealthy gave "out of their leftovers; the widow gave out of what she did not even have."[39] They both gave to sustain the temple services, but for the rich, giving such an offering was a religious formality that could be satisfied with a minimum, a token, not of what they could give, but of what they were willing to give. It was not an expression of deep personal commitment to God.

This reestablishes a principle found in the Old Testament and in parts of the New Testament: It is not the amount given but the level of one's commitment to the Lord that makes the offering acceptable before Him. The widow wanted to give an offering, and she brought the only thing she had, two inexpensive coins, trusting that God would provide for her. Her giving was based on a decision; in fact, it was based on a faith in which her gratitude and love for God prevailed. It came from the depths of her being. For the rich, giving had no deep meaning; it was a shallow experience, a formality in which faith in God was inactive.

Offerings and True Benevolence

What we have just stated suggests that true benevolence is more than sharing or giving. It has to do with the inner condition of the person, the spiritual strength of one's love for God. This understanding excludes selfishness from the act of giving. Seeking self-recognition through our offerings is absolutely incompatible with true benevolence.[40] Jesus stated clearly that we are to give without expecting any reward from others, and, therefore, our giving must be quiet and secret (Matthew 6:1-4). He forbids us to call attention to our benevolence because it is a private "transaction" between the individual and God. Jesus rejects selfishness as a motivation in giving because it taints the offering. Benevolence does not take place before others; it happens "before God who . . . will make public, reward, and punish secret deeds in the last judgment."[41] Giving must come from a heart that is disposed to give and should become a natural response to love and faith in God (Luke 6:30). It is no less than an expression of self-denial made for the sake of the kingdom of God.[42] When an offering is given in that spirit, it becomes a reflection, in the human sphere, of God's incommensurate giving (see Matthew 10:8; 8:4).

Offerings and Christian Ministry

Jesus told the disciples that it is a responsibility of the community of believers to provide for their needs: "The worker is worth his keep" (Matthew 10:10). The term translated "worker" is *ergátēs*, which is used in secular Greek to designate a person who works for wages.[43] In the New Testament it is used in some cases to refer to apostles and teachers (see 2 Timothy 2:15). "Worth his keep" seems to stress that the individual should receive appropriate wages.[44] Matthew calls the wages *trophé* (literally, "food"), which in this context could be rendered "support"[45] or "one's keep." The parallel passage in Luke 10:7 uses the word *misthos* = "salary, pay." It is from this saying of Jesus that the church derived its authority to support the gospel ministry through the offerings of church members.

Jesus' teachings on offerings puts the main emphasis on the motivation for giving. Worship provides the occasion for offerings of homage and submission through which the Lordship of Christ is recognized. Our giving is therefore an expression of our full commitment to Him based on faith and trust in Him, a decision of the heart and not a formality. Giving is not to be motivated by a desire for self-recognition, because selfishness and an acceptable offering are incompatible. Our gifts and offerings should come from a heart full of gratitude and love, whose main concern is the promotion of the kingdom of God. Such individuals are at peace with others and provide for the needs of their families. Within the church, offerings are to be used to promote the mission of the church.

Paul and Offerings

In the New Testament, Paul, more than any other writer, is the one who discusses the theology of offerings. He does this in three main contexts. The first is during his discussion of his personal reluctance to accept offerings. The second is when he discusses his reaction to offerings sent to him that he did not request or expect. And the third is in passages where he deals with the collection for the poor in Jerusalem.

Paul's Reluctance to Accept Offerings

Paul renounced his right to the financial support of his ministry by church members. Writing to the Thessalonians, he emphasized the fact that he worked to provide for his personal needs and did not accept offerings from them. Specifically, he states, "We did this [work day and night], not because we do not have the right to such help, but in order to make ourselves a model for you to follow" (2 Thessalonians 3:9). Paul justifies his decision in terms of setting an example for those who were unwilling to work to earn their living.[46] Another reason he provided for himself was to demonstrate that there was no greed in him (1 Thessalonians 2:6-9; compare Acts 20:33-35).[47] At times Paul felt that accepting money could become a stumbling block in the way of the gospel, which probably means that he did not want to give the impression that he was taking advantage of the church (see 2 Corinthians 11:9; 12:14-18).[48]

However, Paul was aware of the fact that he had a right to the financial support of the church (2 Thessalonians 3:9). In 1 Thessalonians 2:6 he tells the church, "As apostles of Christ we could have been a burden to you." He defends this right in strong terms in 1 Corinthians 9:1-18. As an apostle, he argues, he has the same rights the apostles have, rights that the Corinthians have recognized in the case of other apostles.[49] He justifies his apostolic right for support from the churches with several illustrations based on the use of common sense: military service at one's own expense is practically unimaginable; a farmer has the freedom to eat from the grapes he planted; and a shepherd has the right to benefit from the milk of his flock (verse 7).

Paul also appeals to the authority of the Old Testament, quoting Deuteronomy 25:4 and concluding, "If we have sown spiritual seed among you, is it too much if we reap a material harvest from you? If others have this right of support from you, shouldn't we have it all the more?" (1 Corinthians 9:11, 12). To this he adds an argument from the sanctuary services: The Levites were supported by the tithe, and the priests were supported by the tithe of the tithe and portions of the sacrificial offerings taken to the altar (verse 13). Paul is using the Old Testament law of tithing as a model for Christian giving.[50] According to Paul, the Old Testament regulation was supported by Jesus Himself: "In the same way, the Lord has commanded that those who preach the gospel should receive their living from the gospel" (verse 14). The phrase "in the same way" states that the Old Testament rule is valid not only for the Jews but for Christians.[51] The Lord commanded the church to apply the same rule to support the ministry of the church. The verb "to command" is a translation of *diatássō,* which means "to order," "to issue an edict," or "to charge with."[52] It designates an official and authoritative declaration, in this case from the Lord.

Paul's refusal to accept offerings was not a rejection of the biblical practice supported by the Lord and that had become an accepted practice in the church for the support of the gospel ministry (see 1 Peter 5:2). He was simply using his freedom to proclaim the gospel without expense to the Corinthians in order to protect the integrity of his apostolic ministry.

Paul as the Recipient of Offerings

Not all Gentile churches accepted Paul's decision to labor in the proclamation of the gospel without receiving payment. In spite of his reluctance, the churches in Macedonia supported him while he was at Corinth (2 Corinthians 11:9). It is in Philippians 4:10-19 that Paul analyzes the impact and meaning of the generosity of the Macedonians.

While in prison Paul received the visit of Epaphroditus, a messenger from the churches in Macedonia. He brought with him an offering from the churches for Paul. In the epistle to the Philippians Paul discusses the significance of this offering and states several important things.

First, the offering from Macedonia was an expression of concern or interest in Paul as a preacher of the gospel (Philippians 4:10). The verb *phroneō* translated "to be concerned" is a difficult one to render into English. It combines the ideas of thinking and sympathy, or emotional attachment,[53] the intellect, and the will.[54] It does not simply mean to think about someone but to be sincerely interested in, and willing to do something for that person. This type of concern seeks an opportunity to express itself in a tangible way. The offering of the Macedonians was not the result of an emotional outburst, but was based on a rational analysis, on the recognition of a real need in one with whom they were emotionally and spiritually united and with whose mission they could identify. They cared for Paul in thought and action, and the offering was the proof of this deep concern.[55] This would suggest that an offering ought to be the expression of a serious concern and interest in the well-being of the church and in the fulfillment of its mission.

Second, through this offering the Macedonians participated in Paul's afflictions (Philippians 4:14). The afflictions are the trials experienced by Paul in the preaching of the gospel. The verb *sunkoinōneō* is related to the noun *koinonía* = "fellowship, participation," and means "to participate/share with someone." The basic idea of the verb and the noun is "to have something in common with someone," making it possible for them to have communion and fellowship.[56] The Macedonians participated in the trials of Paul, made them their own, and deprived themselves of something in order to give an offering.

Paul participated in their well-being by receiving their offering. Thus, they were united in purpose and experience. Offerings become and create a bond of sympathy and love among believers. Paul's ministry became their ministry too.[57] The Macedonians became partners with Paul in "his imprisonment and suffering, although they were many miles removed from him. They had taken some of his burden upon themselves in their genuine and deep sense of concern that expressed itself in constructive action on behalf of the apostle, and therefore on behalf of the gospel."[58]

Third, the offering of the Macedonians was credited to their account (Philippians 4:17). It is significant to notice that for Paul the value of this offering was not based on the fact that it supplied a need he had, but rather in the benefit it contained for the Macedonians themselves.[59] The credit/profit/fruit in their account was growing, increasing. Paul is using commercial terminology to describe the spiritual blessing received by those who give. The material investment produces great spiritual dividends in the lives of the givers.[60]

Fourth, the gift of the Macedonians to Paul was an acceptable gift to the Lord (Philippians 4:18). The true recipient of this offering is God, not Paul. Paul expresses this idea by referring to the offering in sacrificial language: it is a fragrant incense, a sacrifice acceptable and pleasing to God. The offering has been removed, so to speak, from the sphere of secular benevolence and interpreted in terms of its spiritual significance. It not only unites them to Paul but also serves to strengthen their relationship with God. An important principle is conveyed here: "Whatever is done for the servant is in reality done for the Master; whatever is given to a child of God is given to God Himself" (compare Matthew 10:40-42).[61] The support of the evangelical ministry and the mission of the church through one's offerings is always a spiritual experience.

Fifth, the offering of the Macedonians witnesses to the fact that God supplies the needs of the giver (Philippians 4:19). The churches in Macedonia were not rich in material possessions (2 Corinthians 8:2); yet, they gave. Philippians 4:19 seems to be both a prayer and a statement of fact, an expression of trust in God's concern for His people.[62] Those who give offerings are not overly concerned with their own needs because God's love is powerful enough to sustain them. By referring to God as a giver, Paul is indicating that the true motivation for human giving is to be localized there. God provides for the Macedonians and uses them to supply Paul's needs.

Paul accepted this offering reluctantly and proceeded to inform the Macedonians that he had received it: "I have received full payment and even more" (verse 18). Here he uses another term from the world of business transactions. The verb *apechō*= "I have received" means "I have received in full" and functions as a receipt. In New Testament times this verb was written at the bottom of a receipt to indicate that the amount was received, or paid, in full.[63] Here in verse 18 "Paul presents what amounts to a receipt for the collection which the church at Philippi had sent him."[64] The implication is that those who give an offering should be informed that it was received, recorded, and used as indicated. Here we discover an element of accountability on the part of those who receive the offering.

The offering of the Macedonians was a manifestation of true concern for Paul and his apostolic ministry. It united them with him in his trials and in the fulfillment of his mission. It also enriched their spiritual lives because it was given primarily to God and not to Paul. Their giving was preceded by God's giving and concern for them. Paul kept proper records of their offering and sent them a receipt.

Paul and the Collection: A Special Offering

Paul's theology of offerings surfaces in a very particular way in his discussion and interpretation of the collection he gathered among the Gentile churches for the church in Jerusalem.[65] This special offering was so important that he mentions it in several of his epistles (Romans 15:25-28; 1 Corinthians 16:1-4; and 2 Corinthians 8, 9). To clarify its theological meaning and relevance, we will examine the concepts and principles Paul associated with this offering.

Motivation for Giving

In addition to the obvious need of the church in Jerusalem, Paul provides for us a series of statements that seem to give a theological motivation for giving to the collection:

A. God's Gift of Grace: In 2 Corinthians 8:1, Paul points the Corinthians to the grace of God given to the churches of Macedonia, which moved them to contribute to the collection. This could be interpreted to mean that God's grace worked in them, creating a disposition to give, or that God's saving grace reached those churches as a gift through the proclamation of the gospel. In this last case, the fact that God gave His Son as an act of grace for the salvation of the Macedonians motivated the giving.[67] But both ideas are correct in the context. The Macedonians gave an offering because God's grace manifested itself in Christ as a gift of salvation, and that same grace was working in their hearts.[68]

B. Christ's Example: In 2 Corinthians 8:9, Paul summarizes the content of a message that he developed in Philippians 2:6-11: "For you know the grace of our Lord Jesus Christ, that though he was rich, yet for your sakes he became poor, so that you through his poverty might become rich." Christ's willingness to give everything up for the church was a sublime revelation of love, which should motivate the Corinthians to give an offering for the poor in Jerusalem.[69]

C. God's Blessings: Paul reminds the Corinthians that God's abounding grace can provide for them what they need in order to enable them to give (2 Corinthians 9:8-11). Notice that the divine giving originates in God's grace and is not a reaction on God's part to the offering of the Corinthians; God is not paying them back.[70] His blessings are acts of grace that provide the opportunity for the Corinthians to share what they graciously received from the Lord.

The divine blessing, Paul says, results in *autarkeia* = "self-sufficiency": God will provide for all their needs (verse 8).[71] Paul is associating self-sufficiency with economic wealth. But self-sufficiency is for him a gift from God and not, as was believed in some contemporary schools of philosophy, the result of earnest self-discipline independent from God and based on an attempt to live in harmony with reason.[72] In Philippians 4:12, 13, he affirms independence from external circumstances or self-sufficiency on the basis of his reliance, or dependence, on God's power, which strengthens him.[73] Paul also understands self-sufficiency as being enabled by God "to relate more effectively to other people, not to withdraw from them,"[74] by assisting them when in need. Paul seems to consider financial self-sufficiency as attainable because wealth and God's grace are not necessarily mutually exclusive. According to him, "wealth should be viewed as a gift of God's beneficence rather than as a result of a purely human achievement."[75] The offering of the Corinthians should be motivated by the conviction that it is God who provides enough for them to share with others. In this way they are encouraged to overcome selfishness.

Planned Giving

Contributing to the collection was not to be an accidental act but a well-planned one. Paul mentions at least three important elements in the organization of the offering:

A. Based on One's Income: Paul does not require a specific amount of money from each church member, but utilizes a biblical principle to be used by all when deciding how much to give; "according to your means" (2 Corinthians 8:11). What the person has (verse 12), that is to say, the way the Lord has prospered the individual, should be the criterion to be used in making that decision (1 Corinthians 16:2). This is obviously a personal and private matter.

B. Set Apart at Home: The idea of setting apart at home the amount to be offered is suggested in 1 Corinthians 16:2: "On the first day of every week each one of you should set aside a sum of money. . . ." The phrase "each one of you" could be translated literally "each one of you for himself," and suggests something done privately at home. Setting the offering apart was a family matter.[76] In the Old Testament, offerings were set aside or consecrated at home and were taken to the temple at a later time. This seems to be what Paul is suggesting.

C. Given to Appointed Instruments: Paul was conscious of how important it was for the church members to know and be assured that the collection would be handled properly. An accidental mismanagement of the offerings would damage his reputation as a spiritual leader and would give credibility to the accusations raised against him by false apostles. Therefore, he sent Titus, his apostolic delegate, accompanied by two brothers who were well-respected in the churches, to Corinth to collect the offerings (2 Corinthians 8:17-23; 9:3). One of the brothers was elected or appointed by the churches to accompany Titus. He represented other churches participating in the collection (8:19). The Greek word *cheirotonein* = "to elect" meant originally "to elect by a show of hands" and may suggest how this person was chosen.[77] The second brother may have been chosen by Paul or the churches (see verse 22). This person had been tested and shown himself to be trustworthy.

It was to these three well-qualified and reliable persons that the offerings were to be given. They represented the apostle and the churches, suggesting that the offering was not being given to Paul but to the church.

The global offering was to be taken to Jerusalem by persons approved by the church, persons to whom Paul would give letters of introduction (1 Corinthians 16:3). All this was done to avoid any criticism and to do what was right, not just before the Lord but also in the eyes of the people (2 Corinthians 8:20, 21).

The logistics of the collection served several purposes. The church members knew to whom they should give the offering. In addition, an element of accountability was present; Paul was careful to make it clear that the offering was not to be misused or misplaced. As a church leader he was responsible and accountable for the collection.

Attitude Toward Giving

The collection was a freewill offering, but Paul expected that it be given in the proper spirit. He made a special effort to clarify the meaning and significance of this offering.

A. Giving Is a Privilege: Apparently, Paul did not ask the Macedonians to participate in the collection because they were poor. Yet, to Paul's surprise they begged and insisted on "the privilege of sharing in the service to the saints" (2 Corinthians 8:4). The Greek term translated "privilege" is *charis*, which is usually translated "grace," and here it means "gracious act"; that is, doing something that is considered to be a privilege.[78] For the Christian it is a privilege to be able to perform an act of grace toward others. The Macedonians had received the grace of God (2 Corinthians 8:1), and now they considered it a privilege to allow that grace to manifest itself through them by helping others.

B. Giving Willingly: The Macedonians gave their offerings "entirely on their own" (2 Corinthians 8:3). Paul did not ask them to give; they gave on their own initiative. The Greek term *authaíetos* = "on their own" means "voluntarily." Giving should be a free decision of the heart (2 Corinthians 9:7). Giving from the heart means that the offering is not given reluctantly or under compulsion. The term *lupē* = "reluctantly" is usually translated in the New Testament as "hurt, pain." Here it refers to those who consider giving to be painful to them but who do not dare to say no. They give, but they do it reluctantly. The term *anágkē* = "compulsion" means acting under the control or influence of someone or something other than one's own volition. It denies the element of freedom in the subject of the action. Compulsion could be the result of the pressure of the group or of the leader, making the individual feel that she or he does not have any choice but to give.

Giving reluctantly or under compulsion is contrasted by Paul with the attitude of joy that should characterize the giver (2 Corinthians 9:7). It is this inner, positive disposition and not the amount given that makes the gift acceptable to God (2 Corinthians 8:12).

C. Giving Generously: God's *abundant* blessings should move the Christian to give generously (2 Corinthians 9:11, 13). The Greek term aplòtēs = "generosity" is a significant one but difficult to render into English. The common translation is "simplicity, sincerity."

The term is difficult to translate because it bears a range of meanings, which are expressed in English by several different terms. In 2 Corinthians 8:2, the term is used to describe the Macedonians as people of "simplicity, sincerity, uprightness, frankness," as well as "generosity and liberality." Together these terms express the ancient ideal of the simple life. According to this cultural ideal, people who live the simple life can be expected to show generosity in their giving and in their hospitality.[79]

For Paul the simple and generous life of the Christian is an imitation of the attitude of their Lord (2 Corinthians 8:9). At times this generosity expresses itself by giving more than one is able to give (8:3), but Paul expects the Corinthians to give only according to their means. Even so, they should try to excel in giving, to abound in the grace of giving (8:7).

D. Giving and Self-Giving: Paul was impressed by the unexpected involvement of the Macedonians in the collection and credited their unselfish disposition to the fact that "they gave themselves first to the Lord and then to us" (2 Corinthians 8:5). Every offering is, in a sense, the offering of the individual in consecration to God and in service to His church ("us"). Hence, an offering is the embodiment of a disposition of the heart, of our willingness to surrender and consecrate our lives to the Lord.[80]

Purpose of the Collection

The first and most obvious purpose of the collection was to supply the material needs of the church in Jerusalem (Romans 15:26; 2 Corinthians 9:12). But this was not a simple act of social benevolence. Paul refers to it as "a service" (*leitourgia*), and although that term is used in Greek literature to designate a service performed at one's own expense in a nonreligious sense, the context of 2 Corinthians 9:12 indicates that it is being used by Paul in a religious sense, meaning "service, worship." The offering given to supply the needs of the church in Jerusalem was an act of worship to the Lord.

The second purpose of the collection was to strengthen the unity of the church and to give expression to it in an objective way. It was "a tangible expression of the unity of Jews and Gentiles."[81] The Jews shared their spiritual blessings with the Gentiles, and now the Gentiles share their material blessings with the Jews (Romans 15:27). There was only one church, a universal one, characterized by a spirit of true fellowship in Christ. Paul perceived that it was necessary for the world church to express its unity in message and mission, and he found in this offering a channel through which this could be accomplished. The material and spiritual blessings of the churches belonged, so to speak, to the one church of Christ.

The third purpose of the collection was to promote financial equality (2 Corinthians 8:13-15). This is the equality produced by "the balance of scarcity and plenty which should exist among the churches."[82] The underlying concept is the one of partnership, *koinōnia*, suggested in Acts 2:44, 45.[83] It is useful to observe that Paul is basing his argument on a passage from the Old Testament: "He who gathered much did not have too much, and he who gathered little did not have too little" (Exodus 16:18). The call to equality is based on the understanding that it is God who provides what is needed. By sharing their blessings, the believers work with God in the creation of financial equality in the church. Those who have plenty are to share with those who have less "that there might be equality" (2 Corinthians 8:13). The equal distribution of wealth may not be a possibility in the world, but it should be a reality within the church.

The fourth purpose of the collection was to express Christian love. Participating in the collection was a test of the sincerity of the Corinthians' love (2 Corinthians 8:8; compare verse 24). This is closely related to the unity of the church, because love binds the church together in Christ. The offering provides the occasion for love to move from the realm of a concept or idea to the arena of Christian behavior as an active principle. The Corinthians had promised to participate in the collection, but had not made that promise true. Now Paul challenges them to demonstrate that love in action (2 Corinthians 9:1-5).

The fifth purpose of the collection was to praise God. Paul

said that the offering "is overflowing in many expressions of thanks to God" (2 Corinthians 9:12).[84] Because it would bless the believers in Jerusalem, the offering would provide a reason to praise God (verse 13). The ultimate purpose of every offering should be to glorify God, because through our offerings we confess that He is the One who provided the means and created the willingness in the human heart to give. Generosity will result in acts of thanksgiving to God (verse 11).

By reminding them about God's grace, which they received freely (without charge), by pointing them to Christ's self-sacrifice, and by assuring them of God's constant love manifested in the blessings they received every day, Paul motivated the Corinthians to give their offerings. For Paul, giving was a privilege, because God's grace was using those who gave. This meant that an offering should be given from the heart and should be a joyous experience. It should be generous, and in a very special way it must be an act of self-giving. An offering, according to Paul, was a means of supplying the needs of the church, but it also contributed to the church's unity and financial equality. Through the collection, Christian love was expressed and God was to be praised. The offering was to be based on the financial situation of the family, to be set aside at home, and then to be given to the church's appointed instruments at the appointed time. Proper management of the funds was expected of those who handled the collection.

Offerings in Acts

The book of Acts mentions some of the financial problems confronted by the apostolic church as it developed and grew to become a world movement. Although Acts does not say much about offerings, it would be useful for our purpose to examine the pertinent passages. Those passages show a particular interest in offerings for the poor of the church.

Offering for the Poor

According to Acts 2:44, the members of the apostolic church had "everything in common"; that is to say, their possessions were at the service of the church and its mission. This should not be understood to mean that they sold *everything* they had and gave the money to the church. What is said is that as need arose from time to time, they sold some of their properties to provide for the needs of others (Acts 4:34, 35).[85] Therefore, this practice was not a rejection of private ownership but rather its recognition balanced by a disposition to serve others.[86] This was necessary because at that time a number of the new converts were poor. This practice was probably a perpetuation of the fraternal community life of Jesus and His disciples (compare Luke 8:3; John 12:4-6; 13:6-9).[87]

Two specific examples are given of the practice followed by the church. Barnabas had a property and decided to sell it and bring the money to the church to provide for the needs of the poor (Acts 4:36, 37). He sold the property and brought the money to the disciples. The second example is the one of Ananias and Sapphira (5:1-11). They made a similar promise, but after selling the piece of property decided to retain some of the money secretly for themselves. Yet, they wanted to give the impression that they were bringing the full amount to the apostles.

The experience of Ananias and Sapphira reveals several important aspects about this type of offering. First, the donation was not just a social act of benevolence but an offering brought to the Lord. The one who ultimately received it was the Holy Spirit. This explains why Peter said to them, "You have lied to the Holy Spirit" (Acts 5:3). Second, the offering was a voluntary one; no one was forced in any way to sell a piece of property. Apparently, after selling the property, Ananias and Sapphira had the option of keeping the money for themselves, if they would be honest with the apostles (Acts 5:4).[88] Third, once more we witness the fact that in giving an offering the right motivation is of primary value. In the case of Ananias and Sapphira, disposing of the land was motivated "by a desire to gain reputation for generosity rather than a genuine concern for the needy among them."[89] Their selfishness, manifested in an unruly concern for their financial security, led them to violate a pledge made to the Lord. The Holy Spirit, who was guiding the believers and the church, was rejected by this couple, and, in turn, He rejected them too. Finally, this incident indicates that it is right and important to pledge offerings to the Lord, but it is equally important to fulfill those pledges.

The procedure followed in the collection and distribution or use of the offering was simple. The believers decided by themselves to sell a piece of property and pledged to give all the money, or perhaps a part of it, to the church. The money was given to the apostles, who were responsible for administering it (Acts 4:37). This may have been the system established by the church and followed by the believers.

As the church grew, it became evident that the apostles could not manage the finances of the church and at the same time proclaim the gospel full-time. They soon discovered that it was impossible to do both things well. The problem became acute when a group complained that some widows were being neglected in the distribution of bread (Acts 6:1-6). This called for a revision of the administrative processes, so the apostles met with all the disciples in the church (church members) and together they approved a new plan. As a result, seven men were elected to be in charge of the distribution of the bread. In the selection process they looked for individuals who were "known to be full of the Spirit and wisdom" (Acts 6:3). In other words, two important qualifications were required. First, they were to be spiritual leaders committed to the Lord and possessed by the Spirit; and second, they were expected to have some knowledge of how to deal with administrative matters, particularly the management of funds.[90] The combination of these two elements indicates that the administration of the finances of the church is not a matter of secular bookkeeping, but it is a deep and essentially spiritual matter.

Some important theological concepts are at the foundation of the offering under consideration. Since most of these concepts have been discussed in the context of other offerings, we will mention them only briefly here. The offering was an overflow of the grace of God in the hearts of the believers and is associated with the statement that "much grace was upon" the believers (Acts 4:33). The implication is that, within the community of Christians, God's grace took the form of a serious concern for the poor in the church. His grace moved them to give. In addition, we should observe the church members' perception of their properties: "No one claimed that any of his possessions was his own, but they shared everything they had" (Acts 4:32). Their concept of ownership was radically modified through the gospel. They knew who the true Owner was. Finally, like the Pauline collection, the offering was a testimony to the unity of the church; they were "one in heart and mind" (Acts 4:32). They had one Lord, one faith, one baptism, and one God (compare Ephesians 4:4, 5)—they were one in Christ, and this was demonstrated "in their readiness to meet one another's need."[91] Spiritual unity expresses itself in tangible manifestations of love, and in this particular case the offering played that role.

Special Offerings

Acts 11:27-30 makes reference to a special offering sent by the church of Antioch to Jerusalem. This was another voluntary offering. The prophet Agabus foretold the coming of a severe famine to the Roman Empire, and this moved the church "to provide help for the brothers living in Judea" (Acts 11:29). This was a special fund to be used in the coming emergency. Each one gave what he or she could afford, and the offering was given to Barnabas and Saul to take to the church in Jerusalem. The offering "was motivated by the love of Christ, expressed the solidarity of the Christian fellowship, and showed that God had received the Gentiles into the church. The congregation at Antioch did not think of itself as isolated from the mother church in Jerusalem. It thought it only natural to send help to another part of the body that was having difficulty."[92] This offering may have provided for Paul the theological model he used for his collection for the church at Jerusalem.

Acts tells us that the church members put their possessions at the service of the church. This was based on their understanding that God was the real owner of whatever they had. Their willingness to give was the result of the work of God's grace in their hearts. Those whose offerings were motivated by selfishness were rejected. The offering was given to God, although it was received by His human instruments, the apostles. The administration of the funds was placed in the hands of capable persons who knew about management and who were also spiritual giants in the church.

Summary and Conclusions

We have examined a good amount of biblical material dealing with the subject of offerings, and it is time now to summarize our conclusions. Practically every passage we studied made its own contribution to a better understanding of the meaning of offerings. In most cases we detected a number of underlying themes that show up quite often in the discussion.

The *theological foundation* of the practice of bringing offerings to the Lord seems to be formed by three main and interrelated theological concepts. The first is soteriology; that is, God's constant and loving disposition to save humans from the power of sin. Salvation is a revelation of God's grace and reaches us as an undeserved gift to be accepted by faith in Christ. God's self-revelation disclosed the unfathomable fact that He is the Greatest Giver in the universe. In the Old Testament, God's disposition to save was manifested in a particular way in the Exodus when He redeemed His people from the enslaving power of Egypt. In the New Testament, God's salvation reached its ultimate manifestation in the gift of His Son as the only means of salvation. The Father and the Son made grace available to those who, through faith in Christ, accepted the gift. God provided the offering that no other person could provide. Human giving is a pale reflection of God's giving.

The second element in the theological foundation is God's faithfulness to His promises, the constancy of His word. Inconsistency of word and action is foreign to the Divine Being. He promised to dwell with humans, providing them with an identity and supplying their needs, and He fulfilled His promises. The Lord is reliable and dependable. His creatures can wait on Him and rely on Him. There is a constancy in the divine character that makes God trustworthy. He is faithful to Himself, to His own character.

The third element in the theological foundation is God's Lordship. The God who saved us freely and who is faithful to His promises is also our Lord. He entered into a covenant relationship with us, accepting us as His people, and we accepted Him as the covenant Lord. His Lordship is not restricted to the realm of spiritual matters, but includes in a more concrete way the recognition that everything we have is His because He gave it to us. God's Lordship means that He is the Owner but that He is naturally disposed to give of what is His to His people. Therefore, whatever His people possess reaches them as a gift or a blessing from the covenant Lord.

In addition to other elements, the three theological foundations that we have discussed provide *the motivation* for human giving. Humans are called and challenged to give because God's grace revealed itself in the free gift of salvation through Christ. Christians possess the sublime example of God and His Son as models of benevolence. Our giving is to be patterned after the divine. Created in God's image, humans are to imitate the divine disposition to give. Since God gives freely, humans should also give freely.

Christians are motivated to give because God, who keeps His promises, is constantly blessing and protecting His people. Those blessings reach us in different ways, but He is always blessing us. God, therefore, is not a person who gave in the past and gives no longer. It is through His providential giving that He is preserving His creation. The fact that He is constantly giving provides a model and reason for human giving. Hence, no one should come to worship Him empty-handed.

The recognition of the Lordship of God should be a motivating factor in our giving. Those who perceive themselves as owners will not likely give out of love. The recognition of the fact that there is one Lord who rules the universe and owns everything in it lies at the root of benevolence. God wants to use us in the administration and proper distribution of His goods. In that theological setting we can only see ourselves as His stewards, who joyfully use what He has given us to promote His plan.

Another motivation for giving is found in the recognition that God is working through His church for the salvation of humanity. He brought the church and the gospel ministry into existence to continue to reveal His glory to the world. Those in the apostolic church found their greatest joy in the promotion of the cause of God through their offerings. Nothing was more important for the believers than the proclamation of the gospel, and they counted it a privilege to be instruments of God in that task. Telling others that God was reconciling the world to Himself in Christ was so meaningful to them that, at times, some Christians gave offerings beyond their resources.

In summary, we could say that what motivates Christians to give offerings is their love for God, a selfless love whose focus of attention is God and fellow human beings. Giving motivated by a thirst for self-recognition is out of place in the Christian life. Jesus challenged the believers to give quietly, silently, expecting their reward from God. Selfishness taints the offering and makes it unacceptable to God. Neither should an offering be given to obtain or gain God's sympathy, love, or recognition. It is only through the sacrificial offering of Christ that we are accepted by God.

This last comment leads us logically to a definition of an acceptable offering. Several elements appear in the Bible to help us define this term. First, *an acceptable offering* is one that is an expression of our self-offering to God. In our gifts we should be giving ourselves to God, renewing our commitment to Him. An offering is to be a deeply religious experience because it is a token of a life wholly surrendered to the Lord.

Second, an acceptable offering is a testimony to the fact that God is first in the life of the believer. Because He has been recognized as Lord, the best and most costly gift is brought to Him based on the person's resources. The offering becomes an act of homage and submission to the One who redeemed us and is now our Lord. By setting aside the offering before using or investing the money in anything else, we are saying to the Lord and to ourselves, "Lord, you are first in our lives."

Third, an acceptable offering is an expression of faith in God's providential care for us. This offering comes from a heart that trusts in a personal God who provides for our needs as He sees them. When an offering is given from one's surplus, it tends to become a formality, a ritual act devoid of devotion. Faith in God is always seeking a way to express itself, to make itself meaningful. Our offerings provide one possible channel to express our faith in a setting of worship.

Fourth, an acceptable offering is the embodiment of the worshiper's gratitude, thanksgiving, joy, and love. These are all responses to the experience of God's redemptive and providential love. In biblical thinking, the inner being discloses its nature and purpose through actions. The positive responses to God's love express themselves in different ways in the lives of the believers, and one of those ways is through a tangible offering accompanied by a confession of the goodness of the Lord. An offering is the shape that our inner feelings and attitudes toward God's love take in the act of worship.

Fifth, an acceptable offering is a freewill offering. An offering is not to be brought to the Lord under compulsion or reluctantly, but voluntarily. The fact that the Lord expects and requires us to give offerings should not lead us to conclude that this is another burden for the believer. God wants us to experience the joy of giving, which enriches our lives.

Sixth, an acceptable offering reflects our commitment to the message and mission of the church. Since we believe that God is using His church to proclaim the gospel and to prepare the world for the second coming of Christ, we should be willing to put our financial resources to the service of God's plan for humanity. This means that in giving our offerings to the church, we are indeed giving them to God to promote and develop the last aspect of the plan of salvation. No greater cause can be found on earth to which we can commit the resources we have received from our Lord.

Seventh, an acceptable offering is one that comes from a heart at peace with God and others. The act of worship presupposes that religion and ethics are not to be compartmentalized or separated from each other. Dealing properly with others is as much a religious duty as bringing an offering to God. In a special way, treating others fairly means providing for the needs of our relatives. Zeal for God and His cause should never lead Christians to give offerings to the Lord that would result in the neglect of the needs of their families. Providing for them is also part of our religious duty.

Finally, an acceptable offering, although spontaneous, is at the same time systematic. We are expected to plan our giving based on our income. The amount to be given is to be set aside at home, with the family, and then brought to our church and given to the Lord. This protects us from a form of giving that is based on emotional motivation.

Our last point raises the question of the logistics in the biblical system of offerings. The Bible provides certain guidelines in *the collection and management of offerings.* We mentioned already that the amount is based on the blessings received from the Lord and that it was to be set apart at home. In addition, God and the church appointed specific instruments (persons) to receive the offerings. They were to be given only to those recognized by the community of believers as being worthy of receiving and administering them. The place to bring them was the temple or the church where people gathered for collective worship to the Lord. There is some evidence to the fact that proper records were kept and that the offerings were used for the assigned purposes.

The Bible mentions several *specific purposes* for bringing an offering. The first is to support the needs of the sanctuary in the Old Testament and the needs of the church in the New Testament. Thus, we find offerings for the building and reparation of the sanctuary temple, offerings for the poor, and offerings for the support of the sanctuary services and the gospel ministry. The offerings were used to contribute to the fulfillment of the mission of the church as God's instrument in a world of sin. They kept the local and the world church functioning.

Second, the purpose of the offerings was to strengthen the unity of the church. Through their offerings believers showed themselves to be one in spirit, message, and purpose. By supporting a local project, the world church found an occasion to express the unity that kept them together. The burden and trials of one congregation became the burden of the whole church. The believers throughout the world identified themselves with the needs and trials of those laboring in specific places.

Third, the purpose of the offerings was to create financial equality in the church. Those who had much shared with those who had little. God's blessings may differ from person to person, but He expects those who have received much to assist Him in creating a balanced distribution of wealth. Such equality will take into consideration both local and world needs.

Fourth, the purpose of offerings was to motivate people to praise God. Through our offerings the spirit of gratitude is nurtured within the community of believers, and God, is praised because of the benevolence of His instruments. Offerings should stimulate others to praise God who through His grace created a spirit of liberality in the hearts of the givers.

We should look briefly at the system of offerings from God's perspective. What was God trying to accomplish in the believer through the request for offerings? There is a strong spiritual benefit for those who bring their offerings to the Lord. The Bible suggests that God used the system of offerings to teach His people how to express their love and gratitude to Him. He who called us to love Him and our fellow humans, established, among other means, the giving of offerings as a vehicle through which we actualize that love. In this way selfishness is defeated in our lives.

Another reason God required offerings was to keep His people from idolatry. Bringing their offerings to Him reminded them that Yahweh was the true Owner of everything and that it was He who blessed them. The land did not belong to Baal, and it was not Baal who made it fruitful; it was the Lord Yahweh. Every time an offering was brought to the Lord, idolatry was being rejected.

Finally, God required offerings from His people in order to strengthen their relationship with Him. This is, in a sense, the other side of the previous point. Each offering provided the people of God an opportunity to consecrate themselves to God anew. The relationship established with Him through His glorious act of redemption was renewed, and the bond of love was strengthened in an act of personal devotion.

STEWARDSHIP AND THE THEOLOGY OF OFFERINGS

Follow-through Discussion for offerings in the Old Testament

1. Discuss the real purpose behind "sacrificial expiatory offerings."

2. What lessons can be drawn from the fact that animals used for "burnt offerings" were listed on the basis of their financial value?

3. In presenting a "meal offering," what was being expressed?

4. What divine principles can be drawn from bringing God the first fruits of the land?

5. What three principles are illustrated in the "special offering" the Israelites were required to bring three times a year?

Follow-through Discussion for offerings in the New Testament

1. Discuss the implications of the statement: "Seeking self-recognition through our offerings is absolutely incompatible with true benevolence."

2. What was behind the decision of Paul to renounce his right to financial support for his ministry?

3. Discuss Philippians 4:10-19. In spite of Paul's reluctance, why did the churches in Macedonia insist on supporting his ministry?

4. List the spiritual principles in Paul's theology of offerings, as mentioned in Romans 15:25-28; 1 Corinthians 16:1-4; and

2 Corinthians 8 and 9.

5. What lessons can be learned from Paul's insistence that well-qualified and reliable people take the Corinthian offering to Jerusalem?

6. In Acts 4:32, what do we observe was the perception of church members regarding their personal property?

7. What are the three main and interrelated theological concepts behind the practice of bringing offerings to the Lord?

8. Define an "acceptable offering" to God.

9. What specific purposes for bringing an offering to the Lord does the Bible mention?

[The following additional materials on offerings and related topics have been produced by GC Church Ministries during 1991-1994: *Life Principles, SDA Financial Systems, Stewardship and Strategic Planning.*]

Endnotes

1. For the Babylonian religion see Helmer Ringgren, *Religions of the Ancient Near East* (Philadelphia: Westminster, 1973), pp 81, 82, 109-20; and for Egypt consult Siegfried Morenz, *Egyptian Religion* (Ithaca, NY: Cornell University Press, 1973), pp. 87, 88, 94-99.
2. This was suggested by Jacob Milgrom, *Leviticus 1-16* (New York: Doubleday, 1991), p 474. For a discussion on the etymology of the noun see Gary A. Anderson, *Sacrifices and Offerings in Ancient Israel* (Atlanta, GA: Scholars Press, 1987), pp 137-144.
3. All Bible quotations are from the NIVerse
4. This is the conclusion reached by C J Labuschagne after studying the usage of the Hebrew verb *nathan* = "to give" in the Old Testament and noticing how often it is used with God as a subject and humans as the object, and how rarely it is said that humans gave something to God. See his article "Ntn," in *Theologisches Handworterbuch zum Alten Testament*, edited by E Jenni and C Westermann (München: Chr Kaiser Verlag, 1971-76), vol 2, pp 138-141 (hereafter quoted as *THAT*).
5. See John E Hartley, *Leviticus* (Dallas, TX: Word, 1992), p 24; and A Noordtzij, *Leviticus* (Grand Rapids, MI: Zondervan, 1982), pp 30, 31.
6. Milgrom, *Leviticus*, p 145.
7. See G J Wenham, *The Book of Leviticus* (Grand Rapids, MI: Eerdmans, 1979), p 51.
8. See Noordtzij, *Leviticus*, p 40.
9. Compare G A F Knight, *Leviticus* (Philadelphia: Westminster, 1981), p 17.
10. See T W Cartledge, "Vow," in *The International Standard Bible Encyclopedia* (Grand Rapids, MI: Eerdmans, 1986), vol 4, p 998 (hereafter quoted as ISBE).
11. See Leonard J Coppes, "*Nadar* make a vow," in *Theological Wordbook of the Old Testament*, edited by R. Laird Harris (Chicago, IL: Moody, 1980), vol 2, p 1309 (hereafter quoted as TWOT).
12. Roland de Vaux, *Ancient Israel: Religious Institutions* (New York: McGraw-Hill, 1961), vol 2, p 417.
13. See G Mayer, "Ydh," in *Theological Dictionary of the Old Testament*, vol 5, edited by G J Botterweck and Helmer Ringgren (Grand Rapids, MI: Eerdmans, 1974), p 428 (hereafter quoted as TDOT).
14. Noordtzij, *Leviticus*, p 83.
15. See Ralph H Alexander, "*Yādāh* confess, praise, give thanks," *TWOT*, vol 1, p 365.
16. Wenham, *Leviticus*, p 69.
17. Hartley, *Leviticus*, p 30, after noting that the portion of this offering burnt on the altar is called "a memorial," suggests that the term "conveys the idea that the person who makes this offering is remembering God's grace in giving him his daily food."
18. See Knight, *Leviticus*, p 18; and R K Harrison, *Leviticus* (Downers Grove, IL: InterVarsity Press, 1980), p 50.
19. See Richard O Rigsby, "First Fruits," in *Anchor Bible Dictionary*, vol 2, edited by David N Freedman (New York: Doubleday, 1992), p 797 (hereafter quoted as

ABD).
20. Ronald B Allen, "Numbers," in *The Expositor's Bible Commentary*, vol 2, edited by Frank E Gaebelein (Grand Rapids, MI: Zondervan, 1990), writes, "Here is where we tend to fall down. Often we find ourselves giving out of our surplus. When there is no surplus, we are not giving to the Lord. Others find that when they give to God of the first of their best, then they wind up with a surplus they had not even anticipated" (p 853).
21. An offering of the first portion of the dough is mentioned in Numbers 15:18-21.
22. Baruch A Levine, *Numbers 1-20* (New York: Doubleday, 1993), p 446.
23. Noordtzij, *Leviticus*, p 233.
24. See J A Thompson, *Deuteronomy* (Downers Grove, IL: InterVarsity Press, 1974), p 254.
25. See Peter C Craigie, *The Book of Deuteronomy* (Grand Rapids, MI: Eerdmans, 1976), p 320.
26. Mention should be made here of the law of the firstborn of humans and animals, according to which all firstborn belong to the Lord (Exodus 22:29, 30). This was not an offering but a legal requirement from the Lord (Leviticus 27:26). The firstborn belonged to the Lord, and by giving it back to Him the Israelites were reminded of their redemption from Egypt and of their election as God's firstborn (Numbers 3:13; 8:17; Exodus 4:22; Jeremiah 31:8, 9). The firstborn of humans and of unclean animals were to be redeemed (Exodus 13:13; 34:20; Leviticus 27:26, 27). Consult M Tsevat, "Bechôr," *TDOT*, vol 2, p 126.
27. See Philip J Budd, *Numbers* (Waco, TX: Word, 1984), pp 332, 333.
28. Walter C Kaiser, "Nāsā,'" *TWOT*, vol 2, p 602.
29. This offering may have been instituted by Moses. See 2 Chronicles 24:9 and Exodus 30:11-16; 38:25, 26; cf Nehemiah 10:32.
30. See Levine, *Numbers*, pp 247, 256.
31. See Anderson, *Sacrifices*, pp 34, 35.
32. On the function of the second tithe within the Israelite theocracy as a means of helping the poor, see our paper "Stewardship and the Theology of Tithe."
33. See W Popkes, "Didōmi give," in *Exegetical Dictionary of the Old Testament*, vol 1, edited by Horst Balz and Gerhard Schneider (Grand Rapids, MI: Eerdmans, 1990), p 321 (hereafter quoted as *EDNT*).
34. See W W Buehler, "Wise Men (NT)," *ISBE*, vol 4, p 1084.
35. See H Balz, "Mágos," *EDNT*, vol 2, p 371.
36. Donald A Hagner, *Matthew 1-13* (Dallas, TX: Word, 1993), p 28.
37. Ibid, p 28. See Ulrich Luz, *Matthew 1-7: A Continental Commentary* (Minneapolis: Fortress Press, 1989), p 137.
38. See C Brown, "Korban," in *The New International Dictionary of New Testament Theology*, vol 2, edited by Colin Brown (Grand Rapids, MI: Zondervan, 1976), p 43 (hereafter quoted as *NIDNTT*).
39. John Nolland, *Luke 18:35–24:53* (Dallas, TX: Word, 1993), p 979.
40. See Robert H Mounce, *Matthew* (Peabody, MA: Hendrickson, 1985), p 53.
41. Luz, *Matthew*, pp 357, 358.
42. See E Earle Ellis, *The Gospel of Luke* (Grand Rapids, MI: Eerdmans, 1966), p 115; and Norval Geldenhuys, *Commentary on the Gospel of Luke* (Grand Rapids, MI: Eerdmans, 1951), p 212.
43. R Heiligenthal, "Ergátes," *EDNT*, vol 2, p 49.

44. See P Trummer, "Axios," *EDNT*, vol 1, p 113.
45. This meaning is found in Greek documents; see James Hope Moulton and George Milligan, *The Vocabulary of the New Testament* (Grand Rapids, MI: Eerdmans, 1930), p 643.
46. Ernest Best, *The First and Second Epistles to the Thessalonians* (New York: Harper and Row, 1972), wrote: "In Thessalonica his [Paul's] point is simply that if he who, as a missionary, had the right to maintenance, had worked for his living why should not the Thessalonians, who have no similar right. The example, of course, is not his renunciation but his manual work. . . ." (p 337).
47. See David J Williams, *1 and 2 Thessalonians* (Peabody, MA: Hendrickson, 1992), p 39. He writes, "It may have been common knowledge that Paul received gifts from Philippi. This may have led some to conclude that he had come to Thessalonica hoping for some more of the same (cf Phil 4:15f). . . . He calls God to witness . . . that greed plays no part in their missionary service."
48. J M Evert, "Financial Support," in *Dictionary of Paul and His Letters*, edited by Gerald F. Hawthorne and Ralph Martin (Downers Grove, IL: InterVarsity Press, 1993), p 296, discusses several reasons for Paul's refusal (hereafter quoted as DPL).
49. See Hans Conzelmann, *1 Corinthians* (Philadelphia: Fortress Press, 1975), p 152.
50. See our paper, "Stewardship and the Theology of Tithe."
51. Conzelmann, *1 Corinthians*, p 157.
52. See Gerhard Delling, "Diatássō," in *Theological Dictionary of the New Testament*, vol 8, edited by Gerhard Kittle and Gerhard Friedrich (Grand Rapids, MI: Eerdmans, 1972), pp 34, 35 (hereafter quoted as TDNT).
53. See Gerhard F. Hawthorne, *Philippians* (Waco, TX: Word), p 22.
54. See J Goetzmann, "Phronēsis," *NIDNTT*. vol 2, p 617.
55. See Georg Bertram, "Phrēn," *TDNT*. vol 9, p 233.
56. See P T O'Brien, "Fellowship, Communion, Sharing," *DPL*, p 293.
57. Ibid., p 294.
58. Hawthorne, *Philippians*, p 202.
59. See F F Bruce, *Philippians* (Peabody, MA: Hendrickson, 1983), p 154.
60. Hawthorne, *Philippians*, p 206.
61. Ibid., pp 206, 207.
62. With Ralph P Martin, *Philippians* (Grand Rapids, MI: Eerdmans, 1976), p 168.
63. See Moulton and Milligan, *Greek*, pp 57, 58.
64. A Horstmann, "Apechō," *EDNT*, vol 1, p 121.
65. For a summary of the scholarly discussion on the historical and theological issues associated with the collection, we refer the reader to S. McKnight, "Collection for the Saints," *DPL*, pp 143-147. It provides important bibliographical information.
66. See Victor P Furnish, *2 Corinthians* (New York: Doubleday, 1984), pp 399, 413.
67. See Hans Dieter Betz, *2 Corinthians 8-9* (Philadelphia: Fortress, 1985), p 42.
68. See Ralph P Martin, *2 Corinthians* (Waco, TX: Word, 1986), pp 252, 253.
69. Betz, *2 Corinthians*, p 61.
70. Furnish, *2 Corinthians*, p 447.
71. Betz, *2 Corinthians*, p 110.
72. See Furnish, *2 Corinthians*, p 448; G Kittel, "Autarkeia," *TDNT*, vol 1, p 466;

B Siede, "Arkeō," *NIDNTT,* vol 3, p 727.
73. P T O'Brian, "Mysticism," *DPL,* p 625.
74. Furnish, *2 Corinthians,* p 448.
75. Betz, *2 Corinthians,* p 110.
76. William F Orr and James A Walther, *1 Corinthians* (New York: Doubleday, 1976), p 356, suggested that the offering was proportional and substantial and that putting it aside was done as a family.
77. See Furnish, *2 Corinthians,* p 422; and Betz, *2 Corinthians,* pp 74, 75.
78. Martin, *2 Corinthians,* p 254.
79. Betz, *2 Corinthians,* pp 44, 45.
80. See H Balz, "Leitourgía," *EDNT,* vol 2, pp 34, 49.
81. Everts, "Financial," p 299.
82. T Holtz, "Isos," *EDNT,* vol 2, p 202.
83. Furnish, 2 Corinthians, p 419.
84. See Martin, *2 Corinthians,* p 293.
85. See David J Williams, *Acts* (Peabody, MA: Hendrickson, 1985), pp 93, 94.
86. See French L Arrington, *The Acts of the Apostles* (Peabody, MA: Hendrickson, 1988), p 54.
87. F G Untergassmair, "Koinos common," *EDNT,* vol 2, p 302.
88. See Williams, *Acts,* p 97.
89. Arrington, *Acts,* p 57.
90. Williams, *Acts,* p 118.
91. Ibid., p 92.
92. Arrington, *Acts,* p 121.